TRUTHSPEAKING

TRUTHSPEAKING

ANCESTRAL WAYS TO HEAR AND SPEAK THE VOICE OF THE HEART

TAMARACK SONG

Snow Wolf Publishing

SNOW WOLF PUBLISHING
7124 Military Road
Three Lakes, Wisconsin 54562
www.snowwolfpublishing.org

Snow Wolf Publishing is a division of Teaching Drum Outdoor School

Song, Tamarack, 1948 –
Truthspeaking: Ancestral Ways to Hear and
Speak the Voice of the Heart

ISBN: 978-0-9894737-6-7

Text design and layout by James Arneson ~ JaadBookDesign.com

To send correspondence to the author of this book, mail a first class letter to the author c/o Snow Wolf Publishing, 7124 Military Road, Three Lakes, Wisconsin 54562, and we will forward the communication; or email the author at info@snowwolfpublishing.org.

Visit the author's websites at www.healingnaturecenter.org, www.teachingdrum.org, and www.snowwolfpublishing.org.

References to Internet websites (URLs) were accurate at the time of writing. Neither the authors nor Snow Wolf Publishing are responsible for URLs that may have expired or changed since this book was published.

ALSO BY TAMARACK SONG

A Forest Bathing Companion
*Learn About Nature's Rejuvenating Powers
On a Healing Nature Trail Walk*

The Healing Nature Trail
Forest Bathing for Recovery and Awakening

Blossoming the Child
A Guide to Primal Parenting

Starting and Running a Transformational Business
A Step-By-Step Guide for Those Who Want to Make a Difference

Becoming Nature
Learning the Language of Wild Animals and Plants

Entering the Mind of the Tracker
*Native Practices for Developing Intuitive
Consciousness and Discovering Hidden Nature*

Zen Rising
366 Sage Stories to Enkindle Your Days

Song of Trusting the Heart
A Classic Zen Poem for Daily Meditation

Whispers of the Ancients
Native Tales for Teaching and Healing in Our Time

Journey to the Ancestral Self
*The Native Lifeway Guide for Living
in Harmony with the Earth Mother*

Extreme Survival Meat
A Guide for Safe Scavenging, Pemmican Making, and Roadkill

CONTENTS

Dedication • *xi*

Imagine • *xiii*

PART ONE

THE WELLSPRINGS OF TRUTHSPEAKING • *1*

Chapter One

Where We Begin • *3*

Chapter Two

The Nature of Truth • *15*

Chapter Three

Truth At Work • *25*

Chapter Four

What Truth Is Not • *41*

Chapter Five

To Know Your Heart is to Know Truth • *55*

PART TWO

THE ART OF LISTENING • *65*

Chapter Six

Listening from the Heart • *67*

Chapter Seven

Intuitive Listening: Tapping into the Universal Language • *83*

Chapter Eight

Listening With Perspective • *93*

Chapter Nine

And Above All, Courage • *103*

PART THREE

THE ROLES OF FEELINGS AND EMOTIONS • *111*

Chapter Ten

Knowing Our Feelings and Emotions • *113*

CONTENTS

Chapter Eleven
Anger Reflux • *127*

Chapter Twelve
Life According to Fear • *139*

PART FOUR
FIXING WHAT SMOTHERS TRUTH • *151*

Chapter Thirteen
Gossip: A Faux Truth • *153*

Chapter Fourteen
Small Talk: Watered-Down Truth • *165*

Chapter Fifteen
Swearing: Truth Gasping for Air • *173*

Chapter Sixteen
Absolutes: Never Say Never • *183*

Chapter Seventeen
Lies: Truth Buried by Fear • *193*

Chapter Eighteen
Humor: Sugarcoated Truth • *209*

Chapter Nineteen
Secrets: The Last Frontier • *219*

PART FIVE
CREATING A TRUTHSPEAKING CULTURE • *227*

Chapter Twenty
Living the Culture • *229*

Chapter Twenty-One
The Culture's Heart • *239*
The Wisdom Keepers • *243*

Glossary • *245*
About the Author • *251*

This is the companion book to *The Talking Circle: The Circle Way to Harmony for Yourself, Your Family, and Your Community*

DEDICATION

In this day, it is the rare person who is in touch with his or her personal Truth. We are born Truthspeakers, yet we flounder at it after we are indoctrinated in games of deception that we call "hiding your feelings," "getting your needs met," and "not rocking the boat."

My full reawakening to Truthspeaking had to wait until I could realize how unconscious I was to my own Truth. Sure, I had heard about Truthspeaking—even fantasized about what it might be like—yet I was young and needed an example to make it real.

Odei Mukwa (Bear-Heart Woman, a.k.a. Janice Schreiber) provided that model. She was one of those rare souls who was still able to speak her Truth—so clearly, in fact, that it shook me out of my slumber. For that, and for other unexpected gifts, she remains a cherished friend from a long-ago, enchanted time.

Twenty years later, I found myself still bumbling at times when I tried expressing my Truth. Old habits die hard; I needed inspiration to go with the awareness and example. It came from my clan sister, Gegekwe (Hawk Woman, or Debi Johnson), who unexpectedly appeared at my door. She mirrored my Truth-denying habits so well that I had only to get past my reactiveness (That couldn't be me!) to begin hearing my Heartvoice. Gegekwe will forever have a kind place in my Heart.

I wish to honor these esteemed Women of Wisdom by dedicating this book to them. May their healing ways touch others as magically as they have me.

≋

IMAGINE

Imagine a place where there are no lies
where gossip is just a meaningless word
and people naturally speak with respect
The air is not laced with cursing
and there is no shame or judgment
The expression of all feelings is welcomed
Even anger and fear are regarded as gifts

In this place, you can trust in another's word
There is no need for doctrine
as each person knows her own Truth
Even without it being spoken
you can read it in her Heart

Everyone's Truth is heard
as listening is valued even more than talking
And each person's voice is held sacred
There is no need to sweeten it with humor
or mask it with doublespeak
They call this, their cherished way of sharing,
Truthspeaking

PART ONE

THE WELLSPRINGS OF TRUTHSPEAKING

I wrote this book for one reason—to incite a revolution of the Heart. For too long we have been taught to say what others would like to hear, and what makes rational rather than relational sense. We have been encouraged to be assertive, but we have not learned how to listen. To tell the truth is our ideal, yet most of us tell dozens of lies every day.

A Zen koan encourages us to speak our Truths without punishing. In the coming pages, we will reacquaint ourselves with a way of life based on the gentle, clear, and heartfelt communication which the American Indian Elders I apprenticed to called *Truthspeaking*.

Notice that I said "reacquaint." You and I already know Truthspeaking: we have a genetic predisposition to be spontaneous, in-the-now beings with astute expressive and listening skills. We evolved the ability as a matter of survival.

It is only since we have become urbanized that we have begun protecting ourselves by suppressing our thoughts and feelings—and defending ourselves from the thoughts and feelings of others. The following four chapters lay the foundations for dissolving these boundaries, so that we can again say what we really mean and hear what people are really saying.

MY WELLSPRING

When I was a child, I got to regularly practice Truthspeaking with the wild animals in the extensive woods and wetlands that

1

comprised my backyard. As a young man, I lived for several years with a pack of Wolves. After that, I learned the human nuances of Truthspeaking from Menominee, Ojibwe, Blackfoot, Hopi, Iroquois, Australian Aboriginal, and Maygar Elders. They taught me much of the terminology and phrasing you'll find in this book. I augmented this organic tutelage with my lifelong academic study of nature, language, anthropology, and indigenous cultures.

CHAPTER ONE

WHERE WE BEGIN

*M*ost important for the Javanese people is to practice Halus, [their term for Truthspeaking], which means being soft, subtle, smooth, polite, and calm. It is expressed in words as well as with your full presence. It is being sensitive enough to read between the lines. With Halus, the more silent you are, the more you hear. A seemingly hidden Truth can then be seen.

It is a very direct form of communication, yet it does not rely on words. To an outsider, what a Javanese person says could sound like something totally different from what she is really expressing. Often a no is a yes, which caused me a lot of annoyance and confusion in the beginning. A lie existed only as long as I didn't understand it.

Yet, I learned to love this way of communication, as I have to be in real contact with those I'm speaking or listening to in order to understand them.

What is Truthspeaking?

The story above is from a student of mine who lived for several years with traditional villagers on Java in Indonesia. She gives us a taste of what we are going to learn in this book about the form of communication practiced by indigenous and traditional peoples around the world, as well as by animals in nature.

To Truthspeak is to state clearly and simply what one thinks and feels. There is no judgment or expectation, no disguise of humor or force of anger. This manner of speech is sacred, because it wells up from the soul of our being rather than from our self-absorbed ego.

The suspension of our integrity that prevents us from Truth-speaking is possible only because we have learned to speak from our heads rather than our Hearts. In our culture, the rational self is esteemed, and we are trained to approach life from the head. However, to know ourselves, we need to get back in touch with our Hearts and listen to our Heartvoice—the Voice of Truth.

When we speak from the Heart, we speak with a clarity that is not besieged by emotion or the ego's motives. Think of the Heart as the place where our thoughts, sensory input, feelings, and ancestral memories sit down together and formulate the balanced perspective that becomes our Truth. This Truth is an authentic and compassionate reflection of the Now.

Just as importantly, when we listen from the Heart, we can connect with the whole person. We are left with a feeling of intimate awareness of the other person's thoughts and feelings. When we listen completely, with open and unbiased ears, we can hear what the person is attempting to say with words—or what he is trying to hide. *We bear witness to his Truth, even if he does not speak it.*

TRUTH IS NOW

When many of us see the word Truth with a capital T, we think of principles or beliefs. This book is about a much more immediate Truth—what I am thinking and feeling right here and now. This is the Truth that ultimately matters in our lives. It is reflected in our immediate feelings. It dictates what we say and it determines how we act. Principles typically have little effect on the moment at hand. Instead of trying to have values and ideals regulate our speech, we can get in touch with our authentic selves and express that authenticity. The tools and techniques presented in this book will help with this.

Why Truthspeaking?

"I'm doing just fine getting my message across," some people tell me. "Why would I want to improve my communication skills?"

"Because it's about more than communication," I reply. "It's about relationship."

I call the improved communication process CAT for short, and it looks like this:

Communication —> Acceptance —> Trust

Clear communication leads to acceptance. When people know what we are thinking and feeling, they can take us for who we are. They don't have to agree with us, but at least there is no doubt or suspicion. This acceptance leads to trust.

This does not mean that we will think, act, or believe as another person might like us to. Yet the person can trust in who we are, based on a sense of knowing that comes from clear communication.

CAT is the foundation of strong relationships. It is the process I'm going to lay out in this book for building self-supporting and lasting relationships. The way to peace, environmental sustainability, and personal fulfillment is through relationship. *If we cannot listen to each other—and trust in what we hear—we will go on being suspicious and exploitative.* Without CAT, we are typically quick to speak and slow to hear. This is one of the ego's favorite defensive-protective strategies. When we practice CAT, we find ourselves naturally doing the reverse: quick to listen and slow to speak. This is the secret of nurturing relationship.

Once we understand and begin to practice CAT, we are likely to discover that it's not all that hard. We are genetically programmed to communicate clearly. All we have to do is recognize and eliminate the learned communication patterns that keep us from doing so. That, as you shall see, is the purpose of a good share of this book.

Where Is Truthspeaking?

For the most part, Truthspeaking is practiced regularly as a way of life by monks and ascetics, and perhaps by the few healing groups, communities and families that have dedicated themselves to emotional honesty and getting in touch with core drives and desires. Derivatives of Truthspeaking, known as *sacred speech*, *nonviolent communication*, *compassionate communication*, *heart-to-heart talk*, and *clear talk*, are practiced in numerous modern cultures. Some Germans call it *auspacken*, which literally translates as *unpack*. When someone wishes to connect with another on a deeper level, she may ask for an auspacken (unpacking) session; or when someone in authority, such as a police officer, wants to cut to the quick, he might say, "Auspacken!"

There is, however, no substitute for Truthspeaking itself. It lies at the core of all other respectful communication techniques and is, I believe, intrinsic to the human experience. In my studies and travels I have found Truthspeaking being practiced to some degree in virtually every culture, whether Eastern or Western, whether Native or modern.

Truthspeaking is a fundamental principle of all the major religious traditions. *Right Speech*, the Buddhist term for Truthspeaking, was given by Buddha as the third principal of ethical conduct in the Eightfold Path. In the Hindu tradition, it is written in the Yoga Sutras that "When one is firmly established in speaking truth, the fruits of action become subservient to him."[1] The Hindu concept of Satyagraha translates as *insistence on truth*. In the Judeo-Christian tradition, Psalm 15: 1-2 states: "Lord, who may dwell in your sanctuary?... He whose talk is blameless...who speaks the truth from his heart." Mohammed is quoted in the Sahih Muslim (Hadith, 4721) as saying, "A man will keep speaking the truth and striving to speak the truth until he will be recorded with Allaah as a siddeeq [speaker of the truth]." The Sikh faith holds speaking Truth as one of its five pillars.

Yet with all of that, Truthspeaking is currently on the Endangered Speech List. Once common to all peoples, Truthspeaking is now rarely heard on a regular basis outside of remote regions where earth-based ways of living are still practiced. The Web of Life[2] is so connected that the fate and fortune of one strand becomes the fate and fortune of the next. When the Buffalo disappeared, so did the Buffalo Wolf. This is also the way of the Web of Sacred Speech: meaningful relationships, trust, and tolerance go extinct along with Truthspeaking.

In our contemporary culture, many people are locked into patterns of victimization, enabling, and placating. This causes them to struggle with unmet needs, secret urges, and compulsive behaviors, along with a general lack of awareness of who they are and why they exist. Political rhetoric, advertising, Hollywood hype, and the staggering number of wounded relationships all reflect the waning of our Truthspeaking heritage.

Even with all of that, Truthspeaking can be resurrected. It is easier to keep something alive than to begin anew. Immeasurably easier. Ask anyone who has experience with campfires in wet weather. For this primary reason, I offer this guide to reclaiming and restoring the rare and beautiful communication style known as Truthspeaking.

My Return to Truth

Occasionally I am asked where I learned my Truthspeaking skills. Let me start with where I did not learn them: it wasn't in classrooms or workshops, nor was it with counselors or clients. There was no one who sat me down and said, "OK Tamarack, I am now going to teach you about Truthspeaking." If someone had done that, it would probably not have been Truthspeaking I was learning, because it is more a way of being than a way of doing. Native People will tell us that we talk too much. To them, communication is feeling, movement and intuition, along with words.

I learned Truthspeaking directly from Native Elders, and from the animals I have lived with, especially Wolves. Among them, in the wilderness, Truth is all there is. To deny or suppress it is to put yourself—your well-being, your sanity, and perhaps your life—at risk. In *The Mountain People*, author Colin Turnbull states that the Ik, one of the last of the African hunter-gatherers, "are perfectly honest about what they do...having abandoned what might conflict with behavior necessary for survival."[3] Truthspeaking comes from real life, where clear communication is vital.

Truthspeaking is our biologically-programmed way of communicating, which naturally comes alive when we live it. I grew as a Truthspeaker by default, primarily because of my immersion in a culture of Truthspeakers. In this day, few of us have the option of living for a decade or two with Native Truthspeakers. Besides, we need help *now*.

Fortunately, there is another option. Our Truthspeaking ability can renew itself if we break the habits and patterns that have suppressed it. We can then begin practicing it, first with ourselves, and then with those close to us. It will then gradually become our habitual—and naturally preferred—way of communicating.

To support that process, I have distilled the essence of Truthspeaking, identified its major impediments, and molded the two together into this book. My intent here is not to teach you Truthspeaking per se because, as I have mentioned, you already know it. Neither is my intent to present it as a practice, such as an anger management technique or a method for improving intimate relationships. Trying to present Truthspeaking as another such skill would be creating a phony construct. Instead, this book is intended to bring you the reawakening experience that would probably naturally occur if you were living with Truthspeakers.

It wasn't until I was a young adult that I encountered Truthspeaking among the Native Elders I had sought out in the quiet places of America, where traditional ways persisted. A few of those Elders I spent as little as a day with, and others I studied under for a decade or more. That was a long time ago, and most of them are no longer alive. Some of their names I never knew or have long forgotten, and others I could never forget, and yet the guidance and encouragement of each continues to echo within me. *"Weweni dibaajimon**—Speak your Truth," was sometimes whispered so softly that I wasn't sure whether it was coming from their lips or through our psychic connection.

These Elders may have been some of the last to remember the time when the Truth of one's Heart flowed as freely and clearly as Snowmelt over Water-polished Rock. Back then, all voices were Truthspeaking voices. Now, like the voice of Truth, the guidance of the Elders who have left us is hard to hear. Through this book, I will use my voice in the hope of making their guidance audible again.

My academic training in psychology, anthropology, philosophy and animal behavior, along with my counseling career (relationship, individual, academic, military draft alternatives), and my education from Native People and Wolves have provided fertile ground for my personal Journey back to Truthspeaking. I have taught and practiced Truthspeaking in family, work, and academic environments for many years, and Truthspeaking skills are the cornerstone to my counseling practice. I pray that some of my stories of struggle and discovery will find resonance with you here.

The Healing Power of Truthspeaking

Above all, this is a healing book. Denial and suppression of our Heartvoices eats away at our insides, causing turmoil that is both emotional and physical. Misunderstandings and reactiveness often result from couching our words for fear of reaction, or from not being attentive to what is being said. If I do not speak directly and to the point, is it fair for me to expect someone to clearly understand me? If I do not listen attentively, can I be sure that I have heard exactly what was being said?

Time and again I have seen people who struggle with chronic anger and victimization-enabling patterns make tremendous

---

* Italicized non-English words in the text are in the Ojibwe language, which is spoken by many of my Elders.

9

strides by doing nothing more than learning how to speak clearly and listen effectively.

As soon as we give our Truth an opening, it will begin pouring forth like a bubbling spring that has just been cleaned of choking debris. The free and spontaneous flow of our Truth is cleansing and uplifting: it reflects in how we take care of ourselves, how we eat, and even our self-esteem. Truthspeaking is the simplest, most direct, and effective path to total well-being that I know of.

Much of the debris that inhibits the flow of Truth comes from the very words we use to convey it. The traditional Hawaiians have a saying, *I ka ʻōlelo no ke ola, i ka ʻōlelo no ka make*[4]—*Life is in speech; death is in speech. I hold speech as sacred because it is a tool of fierce beauty: it can inspire, and it can destroy.*

Thus along with the gift of speech comes sacred responsibility:

- First to understand its power.
- Second, to learn to use it wisely.
- Third, to encourage it in others.

Words are like sticky Spider silk: we often weave them into a web, then walk into it and become entangled. Another option is to step back and take note of the striking, intricate pattern that our word-silks have formed, then look through it to the clarity beyond, rather than getting snared in it. This book is a guide to realizing the power of our word-web, and to using this power to free our thoughts and feelings, rather than being victimized by them.

Our words entrap us in part because we use too many of them. The more words, the tougher the web, and the harder it is to see through it. Realizing the power of words, a Native typically chooses them with intention—and sparingly. Small-talk and gossip are avoided. The Native connects with her inner Truth, and with outer perspective, before speaking. She will do the same when listening to the words of others. This respectful way with words is the lifeblood of Truthspeaking, and it is what will ground our return to it.

Our Journey Forward

Before jumping into the heart of Truthspeaking, I would like to briefly outline what we will cover in this book, so that you may embark on this journey with eyes open.

- **Part I** helps us discern what is and what is not Truth, so that we may distinguish our Heartvoice from the shrewd callings of the ego, the intellect, and emotion.

- **Part II** teaches how to use respectful listening to create a space for Truth to emerge, knowing that in order to become Truthspeakers we must first become Truthlisteners.

- **Part III** shows us how to control the patterned feeling responses that so encourage us to conceal our Truth. When we speak respectfully, avoid negatives, express our feelings, and detach from outcomes, we open windows to clear understanding.

- **Part IV** has us examine how humor masks Truth, how swearing distorts it, how small talk sidesteps it, how gossip creates False Truth, and how lies are actually a form of Truth. We learn how to redirect each of these deviations back to our Heartvoice.

- **Part V** gives guidance on creating a Truthspeaking culture, and it helps us walk Truthspeaking into our lives by distilling it to its essence.

- **The companion book,** titled *The Talking Circle: The Truthspeaking Way to Bring Harmony to Your Family and Community,* gives an envisionment of what can blossom when we take Truthspeaking beyond ourselves and invite others to participate. That title shows how to help Truthspeaking ripple throughout our communities.

I now extend the invitation to you to continue stirring from civilized slumber and join me in reawakening our thirst for Truth.

The Chapter at a Glance

In our culture, the rational self is esteemed, and we are trained to approach life from the head. However, to know ourselves, we need to get in touch with our Hearts and Heartvoice—the Voice of Truth. When we speak from the Heart, we speak with a clarity that is not besieged by emotion or the ego's motives. I call this way of communication *Truthspeaking*.

To Truthspeak is to state clearly and simply what one thinks and feels. There is no judgment or expectation, no disguise of humor or force of anger. This manner of speech is sacred, because it wells up from the soul of our being rather than from our self-absorbed ego.

Truthspeaking is at the core of other modes of conscious communication known as *sacred speech, nonviolent communication, compassionate communication, heart-to-heart talk*, and *clear talk*. I learned Truthspeaking from Native Elders and from the animals I have lived with, especially Wolves. Among them, in the wilderness, Truth is all there is. To deny or suppress it is to put yourself—your well-being, your sanity, and perhaps your life—at risk.

Unfortunately, Truthspeaking itself is currently on the Endangered Speech List. It is rarely heard outside of remote regions where traditional earth-based cultures still exist. As Truthspeaking wanes, so do meaningful relationships, trust, and respect.

Many of us do not realize is that we already know Truthspeaking: we are genetically programmed to be spontaneous, in-the-now beings with astute listening skills. It is only since we have become urbanized that we have begun protecting ourselves by suppressing our thoughts and feelings and defending ourselves from the thoughts and feelings of others. My intent with this book is to help your Truthspeaking ability to renew itself by showing you how to break the habits and patterns that have kept it suppressed.

As soon as you give your Truth an opening, it will pour forth like a bubbling spring that has just been cleaned of choking debris. Much of this rubble comes from the very words we use in trying to convey our Truth.

The traditional Hawaiians have a saying, *I ka ʻōlelo no ke ola, i ka ʻōlelo no ka make*[5]—*Life is in speech; death is in speech. I hold speech as sacred because it is a tool of fierce beauty: it can inspire, and it can destroy.* Thus along with the gift of speech comes a sacred responsibility: to understand its power, use it wisely, and to encourage it in others.

Our return to Truthspeaking in this book will take the following form:

- **Part I** helps us discern Truth, so that we may distinguish our Heartvoice from the shrewd callings of the ego, the intellect, and emotion.

- **Part II** teaches how to respectfully listen, so that Truth can emerge. We learn that in order to become Truthspeakers, we must first become Truthlisteners.

- **Part III** shows us how to control the patterned feeling responses that conceal our Truth. Avoiding negatives, expressing feelings, and detaching from outcomes open the window to understanding.

- **Part IV** has us examine how humor masks, swearing distorts, and small talk sidesteps Truth. It also demonstrates how gossip creates False Truth and lies are actually a form of Truth.

- **Part V** gives guidance on creating a Truthspeaking culture, and it helps us walk Truthspeaking into our lives by distilling it to its essence.

- **The companion book,** titled *The Talking Circle: The Truthspeaking Way to Bring Harmony to Your Family and Community,* shows us what can blossom when we take Truthspeaking beyond ourselves and invite others to participate.

I now extend the invitation to you to continue rousing yourself from civilized slumber and reawaken to your lust for Truth.

Chapter One Endnotes

1 Patanjali, Sutra Number 2.36, Yoga Sutras 2.35-2.45: Benefits from the Yamas and Niyamas.

2 Fritjof Capra, *The Web of Life* (New York: Anchor Books, 1996), 3-17.

3 Colin Turnbull, *The Mountain People,* (New York: Simon & Schuster, 1972), 234-5.

4 Mary Kawena Pukui, *'Ōlelo No'eau, Hawaiian Proverbs and Poetical Sayings.* (Honolulu: Bishop Museum Press, 1983), 129.

5 Ibid.

CHAPTER TWO

THE NATURE OF TRUTH

Truth is a pathless land, and you cannot approach it by any path whatsoever, by any religion, by any sect...The moment you follow someone, you cease to follow Truth. ~ *Jiddu Krishnamurti, Indian philosopher*

Truth is Now, so awakening to our capacity for Truth is awakening to the Now. As the Now continually speaks its Truth, there is neither room nor inclination for those in the Now to harbor secrets. Everything is naturally and spontaneously honest.

All of life dwells in the Now, with the exception of the civilized and domesticated. We have grown accustomed to a different way: watering down our personal Truth before we speak it, in order for it to be accepted. This is because we do not cherish each other for the Truth we speak, but rather for how well we speak what others expect. We thus learn how to communicate everything but the Truth of the Now.

Every time we dilute our personal Truth, we make it harder to ever fully speak it. It's because we are creatures of habit and pattern: the more we repeat a behavior, the more we reinforce it. In addition, whatever we feed, grows, and whatever we ignore, withers.

At the same time, suppressing our Truths sets an example for others, which makes it all the harder for them to be Truth-speakers.

The most sure way to get back on track is returning to where we started—sharing the breath of life in the Now, which is the essence of Truth.

It Begins With Breath

The air we breathe is sacred. It is the breath of our Earth Mother—the breath of all life. It is our vital energy, empowering us and all who crawl and swim and run and fly upon the Mother's bosom. Her breath speaks Her Truth, in order that we may find guidance in it. Her breath then carries our own Truth out into the world. In this way, breath and Truth are One.

Through the breath, we can return to Oneness. Research shows that our breathing rates tend to synchronize when we perform a task together.[1, 2] This synchronic breathing is a form of communication. Bottlenose dolphins use it, as do we when we sigh, yawn, or gasp together. The communicative power of breath is strong enough that two people talking on cell phones in different places will start to walk in sync as a result of cues from their breaths.[3] Even more, some research points to synchronized breathing being a sign of empathy.[4, 5]

Most important to us is the fact that breath is charged with life and is a source of deep connection with each other and our world. The Hawai'ian Natives call the Earth Mother's breath *Ha*. When they greet someone with *Aloha*, they share this breath, and at the same time they share their Truth. Let us do the same with every breath, and let us gift our Truth with every word that we send on the breath.

It is Brevity

Over 100 years ago, Chief Joseph of the Nez Perce said, "It does not require many words to speak the Truth." I have cherished this maxim ever since I first heard it, as it embodies a core precept of Truthspeaking. More recently, "Chief" Luke of the Teaching Drum Outdoor School (where I teach and where Luke is the head carpenter) provided its counterpoint: "It requires many words to keep from speaking the Truth." Taken together, they teach us that our Truth gets easily lost in extraneous verbiage—a misuse of sacred breath.

As a young boy, I remember sitting at the dinner table and feeling uneasy over the silence that sometimes overshadowed our family meals. I felt compelled to fill the void with conversation. It didn't matter about what—I just wanted to hear voices so that I could feel comfortable.

Once, when I was stumbling around for something to say, my father looked across the table at me and said, "If you don't have anything to say, don't say anything."

As young as I was—or maybe because I was so young— I understood, rather than taking it as a directive. Sure, I was uncomfortable with the silence, yet I was more uncomfortable with my assumed responsibility to fill the silence. I recall how I hardly noticed what I was eating when we were all talking, and how much I enjoyed the appearance and smells and tastes of the food when there was silence.

My father was a man of few words. What now impresses me most about his words is that I still remember them. That is because he chose them well. When he talked, he spoke his Truth. His words: "If you don't have anything to say..." have since become for me: "Every breath is Sacred; every breath we are given is for a purpose. Rather than wasting it to fill space, perhaps I can first listen to its voice, then honor its purpose."

It Is a Doorway to Relationship

When we dwell in the Now and use our breath to Truthspeak, we open the door for growth in our relationships. We can stop being afraid of our mate, friend, or parent, and start speaking what we think and feel, *when* we are thinking and feeling it. This simple act, which is so easy yet so hard, is probably the single most magical thing we could do to eliminate the stress inherent in holding secrets. And to find the bliss in everyday life.-

The term *Truthspeaker* can be a bit misleading, as Truth-speaking involves more listening than actual speaking. When we become Truthspeakers, we also open the door to becoming

Truthlisteners. One of the most profound aspects of Truthspeaking to me is that it says, "Let us share our Truths," rather than, "I speak, you listen."

We are products of a culture where the voices of the most dominant and assertive are usually the ones that are heard. Communication is one-dimensional: either we speak or we are spoken to. We often have to fight for our right to speak, or we will not get an opportunity. Many people find the struggle exhausting and dispiriting.

Truthspeaking is based upon a different way of being: the Circle Way. Everything is related; everything is part of the same continual flow. There are no boundaries—giving is receiving and receiving is giving. This is the way it has always been, and still is now, only our civilized culture has obscured it.

In the Circle Way, listening is speaking and speaking is listening. There is no need to create space for myself, no need to drive my point home. Already there is a place for me, just because I am. Inquisitiveness greets my words, not because of what I might say, but because I am valued.

When I speak and listen in this gentle and circular way, I can understand how those raised in the dominant culture could react with confusion, or even irritation and suspicion. There is a world of difference between "I speak, you listen" and "Let us share our Truths." Truthspeaking is the door between these worlds.

I learned how to speak in this honoring way from the Wolves and Doves with whom I lived when I was a youth. Later in life, I continued learning from my Native Elders. They all talked with me in a way that invited me to listen.

Notice that I said they talked *with* me rather than *to* me.

A Dove speaks in a personalized way that attracts the listener to her voice. Even though only she is speaking, the listener feels included, almost as though they were in dialogue. This is because her multi-dimensional language is both expressive and inclusive. Being given that kind of Respect made me *want* to listen, and her soft manner of speaking obliged me to listen attentively. Her honoring tone of voice, which felt like an inviting warm wind, then drew me in completely.

This was Doves' and Wolves' general way of speaking, no matter how serious the subject, and no matter how important it was that I listen. The power of their words came from the spirit of what they were speaking, rather than from intensity or slickness of delivery. This put the onus on me to listen, rather than on them to make sure I *was* listening. As I grew accustomed to their communication style—to Truthspeaking— I came to realize how well it resonated with my life energy and that around me.

AN EASY WAY INTO THE NATURE OF TRUTH

So you do not have a flock of Doves or a pack of Wolves hanging out in your backyard to help you with Truthspeaking? No problem; children will do just as well, and I suspect that they are more common than Wolves in your neighborhood. Children are naturals at Truthspeaking and teaching by example. Their emotional honesty and expressiveness will rub off on us as we become the Now. Try spending at least half a day every week with a child six years of age or under. Older children are more likely to be acculturated, thus less likely to be spontaneous Truthspeakers.

My experience is that as helpful as observing a child can be, interacting with a child can work miracles. There is a saying that the child is the father to the adult. When we come to realize that a child is not just here to be taught, but also to teach, we gain much more than a pristine example of Truthspeaking.

Native Wisdom

Like children, stories can be inspiring teachers. To help bring to life the aspects of Truth and Truthspeaking that we have discussed so far, I would like to share a story that I learned from my departed Ojibwe friend Nick Hockings. You'll find another version, illustrated, in my book *Whispers of the Ancients: Native*

Tales for Teaching and Healing in Our Time (University of Michigan Press, 2010).

There once lived a Woman called Bear-Sees, who felt deep love for a Man known as Looks-Far. The two built their Lodge beside the upriver rapids, where they could serve their People by catching Fish. Soon they were blessed with the birth of a daughter, who was given the name Sees-like-Frog.

One day while checking their Fish traps, Bear-Sees and Looks-Far heard frantic yelps coming from far up the rapids. The cries were so piercing that not even the thrashing water could drown them out.

The pair listened intently, trying to figure out the source of the yelps, which grew fainter and fainter, then faded completely.

Bear-Sees, who was bent over a trap in the knee-deep water, felt something bump the back of her leg. Dropping the Fish she had just grabbed, she spun around to see a Wolf pup, face down in the water. She instinctively picked him up and began to rub him.

After a short while, Looks-Far said, "Did you see that? I think his mouth quivered a little."He is not dead!" exclaimed Bear-Sees, rubbing him more vigorously and pressing on his chest to help him breathe.

Soon he was coughing and wheezing, trying to catch his breath.

Looks-Far then said, "Mother Wolf might have been moving her pups across the stream and slipped on a rock. If she dropped this one, the current may have pulled him away faster than she could grab him."

"It may be that he has come to us because we are intended to caretake him," suggested Bear-Sees. "If that be so, let us raise him as one of our own, and I will nurse him. He is too young to eat and I have milk enough to share with both Sees-like-Frog and him."

"Let us call him Rock-Dancer," said Looks-Far, "in honor of his mother and of the way he came to us."

The next turn of the seasons went peacefully, with both pup and babe growing robust and yearning to explore their expanding world. Much to Sees-like-Frog's delight, it was time for her to leave the cradleboard and take her first steps.

"Look at how they play together, just like sister and brother," said Looks-Far to Bear-Sees one day as they watched the young pair tumbling around in the grass.

"They *are* Sister and Brother," replied Bear-Sees with a warm smile.

One bright morning in the Fish-Trapping Moon, Bear-Sees left to gather Nettle in an upstream meadow. "I'll go down to check the trap I placed in the rapids," Looks-Far said. "Sees-like-Frog is sleeping in the furs at the back of the lodge and Rock-Dancer is on guard outside the door, so they should be fine."

"Yes, they should," agreed Bear-Sees, and they each went their separate ways.

Looks-Far waded out to the trap and reached to open it. Just as he touched the hatch, an anguished scream shattered the morning calm. He froze in place, acutely alert, and a hot surge flashed through his body. His mind raced through a list of possibilities as to where the cry came from.

"No! No—it couldn't be!"

He raced up the bank and burst into the lodge. Standing before him was Rock-Dancer, with blood dripping from his mouth. Pushing past him, Looks-Far scrambled to the back of the lodge. There, in front of a tangled pile of furs, he found his beloved Sees-like-Frog, her twisted body gashed open and lying stone-still in a pool of blood.

Looks-Far spun around, grabbed his hunting club, and sent it crushing into the skull of Rock-Dancer. Over and over he slammed Rock-Dancer, until his wrath was spent. The dazed man then sunk to his knees, let the club fall from his hands, and numbly crawled over to face the horror before him.

As he reached to touch the babe, he caught sight of two sets of bloodied tracks, one Rock-Dancer's and the other much

21

larger. They were from the Cougar who had been lurking around the camp. Looks-Far followed the bloody paw prints to the back of the lodge, where they exited through a hole torn in the wall.

Looks-far read the sign: a fierce but short battle, with Rock-Dancer savagely tearing at the mighty Cougar, who was forced to drop the Babe's lifeless body and escape through the hole he made in the back wall.

The shattered Man stumbled outside, threw his fists to the sky, and let out a wail that shocked everything to mute stillness. Even the river was hushed.

Upriver, the scream slammed through Bear-Sees like a peal of deafening thunder after a blinding lightning strike. She dropped her basket and bolted for home. The fear that only a mother could know roiled in her breast like the fiery core of a volcano.

She reached the lodge gasping so violently that she could hardly stand. There to meet her was Rock-Dancer, his body contorted and his head smashed to a bloody gruel. Turning away from the piteous sight, she caught sight of her mate sitting in the shadows beside the lodge. She then entered the Lodge, her pounding heart making her throb like a drum.

For the second time that awful morning, a soul-rending wail rose like a tidal wave and crashed through the forest, freezing all life in its tracks.

Precious Sees-like-Frog was laid to rest on soft furs in the Passing-over Lodge, and noble Rock-Dancer was placed at her feet, just as they had been in life. Fire was then touched to the lodge, and the flames carried the two siblings over to their Spirit Lodge, where they continued to dwell in the bliss of their sharing.

Bear-Sees and Looks-Far abided in sorrow for a full turn of the seasons. In the final days of their grieving, Bear-Sees suggested, "Let us seek the counsel of the Elders—they say the Gifting Way is everywhere, in everything; maybe they can help us find some small blessing to walk with. We have heaped tragedy upon tragedy with the mindless slaying of our second Child, Rock-Dancer; perhaps through our blindness we can find sight."

The Elders helped them to see that jumping to a conclusion about how their daughter was killed closed them off from Truth. From this, they came to realize that questioning was the only path to Truth.

Soon thereafter, Bear-Sees became heavy with child, and a joy filled their lives that was even greater than when she and Looks-Far first came together. With their newly opened eyes and *Be as a question* as their motto, their family flourished, and their example inspired many to choose the way of Truth.

The Chapter at a Glance

Awakening to our capacity for Truth is awakening to the Now. In the Now, everything is naturally and spontaneously honest. However, we have grown accustomed to a different way: watering down our personal Truth before we speak it, in order for it to be accepted.

We can begin to reconnect with the Now by connecting with our breath. The air we breathe is sacred. It is the breath of our Earth Mother—the breath of life. It is our vital energy; it empowers us and all the animals and plants. Earth Mother's breath speaks Her Truth, in order that we may find guidance in it. Her breath then carries our own Truth into the world. In this way, breath and Truth are One.

The Hawai'ian Natives call the Mother-breath "Ha". When they greet someone with *Aloha*, they share the breath, and in doing so they each share their Truth.

Chief Joseph of the Nez Perce said, "It does not require many words to speak the Truth." More recently, "Chief" Luke of the Teaching Drum Outdoor School (where I teach and where Luke is the head carpenter) provided its counterpoint: "It requires many words to keep from speaking the Truth." Taken together, they teach us that our Truth gets easily lost in extraneous verbiage.

When we dwell in the Now and use our breath to Truthspeak, we open the door for growth in our relationships. We can stop being afraid of our mate, friend, or parent, and start speaking what we think and feel, *when* we are thinking and feeling it.

In civilized cultures today, the voices of the most dominant and assertive are usually the ones that are heard. We either speak or are spoken to. Truthspeaking opens a door to a different way—the Circle way—that says, "Let us share our Truths," rather than, "I speak, you listen."

An easy way into the nature of Truth is to spend at least half a day every week with a child six years of age or under. Older children are more likely to be acculturated, thus less likely to be spontaneous Truthspeakers. Children are naturals at Truthspeaking and teaching by example. Their emotional honesty and expressiveness will rub off on us as we become the Now. Interact with the child, rather than just observing.

Chapter Two Endnotes

1   Gérard Bailly, Amélie Rochet-Capellan, and Coriandre Vilain. "Adaptation of Respiratory Patterns in Collaborative Reading," *14th Annual Conference of the International Speech Communication Association (2013)*.

2   David McFarland, "Respiratory Markers of Conversational Interaction," *Journal of Speech, Language, and Hearing Research* 44, no. 1 (2001): 128-43.

3   R.D. Murray-Smith et al., "Gait Alignment in Mobile Phone Conversations," *AMC International Conference Proceeding Series* 309 (2007): 214–221.

4   S. Ainsworth, "Empathic Breathing of Auditors While Listening to Stuttering Speech." *Journal of Speech and Hearing Disorders* 4 (1939): 139–56.

5   Charles Brown, "Introductory Study of Breathing As an Index of Listening," *Speech Monographs* 9, no. 2 (1962): 79-83.

CHAPTER THREE

TRUTH AT WORK

The story concluding the previous chapter demonstrates the fluid nature of Truth, which allows it to be adaptable and clearly reflective of the Now. The better we understand the three characteristics that give Truth its mutability, the better we can both speak and listen in ways that are faithful to the Now. Here is an introduction to those characteristics:

It Is Direct

In speaking my truth, I directly state my needs and wants. However, this is often easier said than done. When I fear rejection or incrimination, I might couch my need or desire with a question, such as "Do you want to go out to eat tonight?" or "What would you like to do after work?" This amounts to testing the waters rather than speaking my Heart.

A client recently e-mailed me about a man she was seeing who would ask questions like, "Would you like a hug?" or "Would you like to sit closer?" She said she felt uneasy around him because she never knew what he wanted. "I wondered whether he was just a people pleaser, an enabler," she said.

I suggested to her that she speak the same truth to him that she just did to me. Encourage him to say, "I'd like a hug," if that's what he wants. I suggested that she do the same; as it appeared that she was waiting for him to make the first move, which was a passive version of the same thing he was doing.

It Is Personal

According to an African saying, if Lion tells the story of the hunt, it will be different from Zebra's story. It's the same hunt, yet because one is the hunter and the other is the hunted, each of their experiences is radically different. Where Zebra's story would be about her fear for her life and her panicked escape, Lion would tell about her love-inspired quest to feed her cubs. Yet if we heard only Zebra's story, we might get the impression of Lion being a rabid terrorist.

Here is why *Truth is not stated definitively.* Terms like *maybe*, *perhaps*, and *if you wish* are either stated or implied by tone of voice and body language. This creates an opening for others to reflect upon what we share, without feeling constrained by it. At the same time, we create space, support, and encouragement for them to become more aware of their own Truths. Our mutual exchange honors the sanctity of each person's Truth, and so creates an opening for dialogue.

Ohiyesa, a Santee Dakota who grew up in the late 1800s, during the last days of the Buffalo culture, shares the following struggle between those who recognize the personal nature of Truth and those who believe there is a single, universal Truth: "I am reminded of a time when a missionary undertook to instruct a group of our people in the truth of his holy religion. He told them of the creation of the earth in six days and of the fall of our first parents for eating an apple.

"My people were courteous and listened attentively; and after thanking the missionaries, one man related in his own turn, a very ancient tradition concerning the origin of maize. But the missionary plainly showed his disgust and disbelief, indignantly saying, 'What I delivered to you were sacred truths, but this that you tell me is mere fable and falsehood!'

"'My brother' gravely replied the offended Indian, 'it seems that you have not been well grounded in the rules of civility. You saw that we, who practice these rules, believed your stories. Why, then, do you refuse to credit ours?' "[1]

It Is Ever-Changing

We tend to think of Truth as solid and constant, which reflects in our morals, commandments, and laws. Yet, there is an axiom that the only constant is change. We resist that by going through great effort to keep our bastions of Truth established and regarded: we use reward and punishment, shame, social conditioning, peer pressure, and many other methods in our endless effort to resist change.

All of this runs contrary to the natural way of things, where there is continual adaptation to ever-changing conditions. This points to Truth's resilience, not its weakness. It allows Truth-speaking to manifest in a variety of communication styles. If I were to give a person directions based upon mileage and road signs, she would probably find them useful only if she were rationally oriented. Someone who was spatially oriented would do better with audio-visual cues, such as a park, a big tree, or a noisy factory to watch for along the route. The scope and method of my direction-giving change to express a Truth with many personas.

Truthspeaking relies on this attention to context, which involves communicating the circumstances from which I draw my opinions and conclusions. This content helps the listener to know me and why I came to the conclusion I did, while still allowing her to form her own opinions, questions, and perspectives.

In this way, I can offer my Truth from a place of greater perspective, rather than ego. If someone returned from a camping trip out West and told me about how cold and miserable he was while climbing Summit Peak, I could develop a prejudice about Summit Peak. However, if he gave me the context, such as the fact that he was inadequately dressed, and not in proper condition to attempt such a climb, and that he met other people having a better time than him, I would be able to empathize with him and at the same time keep open to the beauty of the mountain.

Far from being indecisive or noncommittal, speaking from a place of greater perspective grants me clarity and conviction. I'm not just describing the Tree I have my nose up against, but also giving you the context of the forest. You'll then better know the tree.

Another reason for this is that this way of communication encourages you to listen, which helps you to know all the more intimately that of which I speak.

To Keep Our Truth Direct, Personal, and Ever-Changing

Speaking our Truth is all we need to do in order to express ourselves. Truth has its own integrity and intrinsic value, simply because it is our Truth.

Yet there are times when some of us cannot trust in this. We might seek validation by trying to get others to agree with our Truth. Statements like "Do you see this also?" and "I don't know what the rest of you think, but I..." are indications that we are fishing for reinforcement. We want to stack up as many versions or acknowledgements of our Truth as possible. This is called *Stacking*.

There are two Truth-squelching sides to Stacking:

1. It depersonalizes our Truth.
2. The people we have engaged to reinforce our Truth give it an inflexibility that inhibits its natural tendency to evolve.

Why, then, do we resort to stacking? Plain and simple, it is fear. I might feel alone with my Truth or unsure about it. I could feel the need to allay my insecurity, bolster my courage, or assert myself. Or I have an ulterior motive and I'm using my Truth—or what I am calling my Truth—as a manipulative tool. Whatever the reason or reasons, it boils down to wrestling with fear.

Once I recognize this, I can separate my fear from my Truth, so that I and others can honor my Truth for what it is. This then allows me to honor my fear by embracing and working effectively with it.

The most common cause of the fear that leads to Stacking is feelings of inferiority. We compensate by continually striving to boost our self-esteem. This drive to appear superior, known as *Narcissistic Personality Disorder*, can be identified by these characteristic behaviors:

- **Flaunting humility**

  "My speech went over well, but it took me a week to write it."

  "I had to sleep the whole next day, but it was worth it because we won the game."

- **Accomplishment crowing**

  "With my double Masters, I was overqualified for the job."
  "I saw through the trick right away."

- **Criticizing**

  "You could have done a better job."

  "Where is his sense of right and wrong?"

- **Upstaging**

  "I wouldn't do it the way she did it."

  "I hope you don't mind that I was invited to sit at the head table."

  "I deserve better than this."

- **Sowing insecurity**

  "Do you think he'll want to date you again?"
  "How did you luck out and finally get a contract?"

Tapping Into Your Truth

Because Truth is personal and constantly changing, it may be difficult to discern whether a need or desire is coming from our Heart-of-Hearts, or whether it is an addictive/patterned yearning. In other words, "How can I tell if I'm Truthspeaking?" The following exercise may be of help. You can do it alone or with a partner. Choose someone you trust and respect, or your ego will put up a boundary to expressing your deepest yearnings.

- Center yourself, in an area free of distraction.
- Ask yourself, "I think I want____; yet what do I *really* want?"
- Ask yourself, "What will that give me?"
- After a slight pause, repeat steps 2 and 3; and keep repeating them until you have reached the bottom. You will know you are there when you feel a sense of peace and knowing.

ANOTHER TEST FOR TRUTH

Whenever I am in doubt about whether what I am going to say is my Truth, I also ask myself, "Is it honoring, and does it foster relationship?" If my answer to both is "yes," I know I am speaking my Truth. And if my answer is "no," I look deeper to find my Truth. I use this easy test every day and it works consistently.

As you practice these exercises, you might want to keep in mind the following exchange I had with a workshop participant, who once asked: "Is speaking my feelings, speaking my Truth?"

"Defining ourselves by our feelings," I replied "is like saying a car needs just brakes to run. Yes, we are feeling beings; yet we are so much more. Just like the car, which needs an engine, wheels, a battery, lights, and so on to run, so do we need our intuition, our senses, our memories, and so on to be complete beings. Truthspeaking, then, cannot be just an expression of our feelings—it is the voice of our Heart, which expresses our total being."

Another tool for distinguishing the voice of the Heart is to ask yourself: "Is what I am about to say in the service of love?" Recently my mate, Lety, was told in a dream that love is the only language. As soon as she told me, I realized that she was just given the most clear and simple guide to Truthspeaking that I had ever heard. You are probably familiar with the saying, *to know you is to love you*. In its most elemental sense, love is knowing. When we speak from our place of knowing—our Heart-of-Hearts—we speak the language of Heart, which is love.

Respectful Speaking and Listening

We are naturally respectful in our speech, and language is naturally honorific. The awarenesses and exercises we have covered thus far allow for these natural qualities of our speech to manifest. Yet these are not the reasons we speak. *As functional social beings, we each hold the responsibility to speak our Truth.*

A good part of exercising this responsibility is carefully choosing words and mannerisms to express our Truth. However, we have been taught from a young age to do the opposite: choose our words to elicit a desired feeling or reaction from others. In other words, we manipulate. To speak Truth is one thing—that takes courage. To do so with respect is another thing—that takes skill.

Our task in returning to respectful speaking is to learn how to communicate in ways that are not laden with guilt, expectation, or judgment. At the same time, we wish to be non-threatening and supportive of another's Truth. This is a tall order, so many simply choose not to communicate.

However, silence does not exonerate us from our responsibility to Truthspeak. Nor does it keep us from communicating. We fill the void by making assumptions, which by definition is still communication.

Only assumptions dishonor our Truth. When we choose silence, we deprive others of the experience of our full Truth, which inevitably leads to misunderstandings and conflicts in relationship.

If relationship matters to us, we need to speak as though it matters. *When we choose not to speak our Truth, we have made the decision that our pride or fear is more important than the relationship.* When we speak our Truth, but do so disrespectfully, we speak from a place of ego. Our Truth then has trouble resonating with others. No matter what beauty our Truth might hold, disrespect gives it a sour taste. Respect is like savory dressing on a salad; it has a way of engendering the trust and empathy that help make our Truth appetizing to others.

Language, being naturally honorific, already contains the ingredients for Respect. Whether or not it manifests depends on what we say and how we say it. The Japanese people have reverential customs for greeting their guests, which include bowing and addressing them in a way that makes them feel honored. A person's choice of words (slang vs. conventional, technical vs. general) reveals the class, education, and status of both speaker and addressee.

The content and the delivery of speech contain codes of either respect or disrespect. This makes it important for us to give content and delivery particular attention. In the long run, how honorable and respectful we are with someone means more to her than whatever we may have talked about. No matter how impressive our factual memory may be, it is still our feeling memory that we rely most upon. *Facts fade; feelings linger.*

Straightforward Ways to Begin Speaking Respectfully

When you and I are able to hold our own Truths, we can then hold each other's. When I know and cherish my own Heartvoice, it is a short step to knowing and cherishing yours. When I can speak with Respect, I can listen with Respect. The experience of this book is first and foremost a personal journey. What we each learn here is best applied to our own awakening before it is shared with others.

Basic Practices:

- **Express rather than repress,** and do it now rather than later. There is a Zulu saying that it is far better to speak your truth with someone while she's still alive than after either of you have died.[9]

- **Be brief and concise.** Talking too long tells others you do not respect their right to speak, nor do you regard what they say.

- **Take thoughts and feelings about another directly to that person.** Sharing them with someone else is gossip (more on this topic in Chapter 13).

- **Avoid absolutes** like *never* and *always*. By using terms like *maybe* and *perhaps*, we acknowledge that things are not always as they appear. Some insects use spiderwebs as roosts, rather than being trapped by them (see Chapter 16 for more).

ABSOLUTES AND HONESTY

Researchers have found that the language of absolutes is marked by lower use of "I" references than speech that is detached from outcome (e.g. "It is possible that...").[2] This finding complements research into language deception which has found that the use of "I" (including "I'm," "I'll," "I've," etc.) is the best indicator of honesty.[3] As we become more self-aware and speak in "I" statements, we become more honest.[4] While Truthspeaking involves our personal and ever-changing truths, the language of certainty is a Faux Truth that is also distinctly impersonal (more in Chapter 16).

Pronouns and Respect

As language evolves, many words and definitions change, yet the meaning of "I" and "you" has stayed the same across languages and generations of speakers. This is so much the case that linguists consider the first-person pronoun to be the world's most stable word.[5] Pronouns in general are also some of the most common words across languages—they account for less than one-tenth of one percent of our vocabulary yet comprise almost 60 percent of the words we use.[6]

One reason for the predominance and stability of pronouns is that they help create resonance in communication. Within 15 to 30 seconds of beginning a conversation with someone, our pronoun use begins to align and even match.[7] Much like the way our breaths can synchronize (see *It Begins with Breath* in Chapter 2), this phenomenon is a subconscious sign that two people are truly listening to each other.

To better communicate our Truths and our respect, we can become more intentional about word and pronoun usage. Here are some suggestions, which I learned from Native Elders and my study of Native languages:

- **Use *who* instead of *that*,** as in "She is the person *who* made the stew" and "I think he is the Crow *who* woke me up this Morning."
- **Capitalize the spellings** of all specific Animals and Plants.
- **Own our feelings,** by saying "I feel…" rather than "You make me feel…"
- **Refer to others before self,** as in "Rachel, Steve, and I gathered berries this morning."
- **Refer to a plant or animal as *she* or *he*** rather than *it*.
- **Refer to oneself as *this person*** or *this woman* rather than *I*—especially when stuck in ego.
- **Use *she* and *he* equally** when in doubt of gender, or use the gender-neutral "they." With a transgender person or when gender identity is unclear, gain clarity by asking the person.

Fearspeaking versus Respectful Speaking

Were there ever times when you feigned respect in order to manipulate someone? What were your reasons? Those I most often hear are:

- To get my way.
- To gain acceptance.

- To protect myself.
- To hide something.

I call this *Fearspeaking*. We communicate half-truths, using words and gestures that are devoid of genuine respect, even though they may mimic it. Inevitably, Fearspeaking backfires, because our essential self knows that it is not real Respect, either for self or other, even if we were able to deceive our audience.

The feelings that Fearspeaking generates don't go away. Instead, they fester and mutate. When they surface—and they will—it'll likely be in distorted and insidious forms that hardly resemble the initial feelings. It could be passive-aggressive behavior, judgmentalism, or any of a number of other abuses.

We can avoid this downslide by cultivating a consistent practice of Respect—first for ourselves, by acknowledging and embracing our Heartvoice; then for others, by speaking our Truth in the Now. Zen scholar Wei Wu Wei states that in order to be effective, Truth must penetrate like an arrow—and it could well hurt.[8] Speaking one's Truth and listening to another's may be unsettling, yet we can temper it with Respect. Avoidance and Fearspeaking only worsen it.

Respect can aid us in defusing and transforming disrespect when it does arise:

- We acknowledge but do not legitimize the disrespect
- We avoid mirroring and encouraging the disrespect we have received.
- We help protect ourselves (and others) from the hurt that disrespect can bring.
- We demonstrate the way of Respect.

I've seen the example of respect play out many times in my life. When someone was angry and swearing at me, and I responded in like manner, I only fed his fury, and he continued on in the same vein. On the other hand, when I responded with kindness and understanding, his energy often transformed and he responded more gently. Instead of pouring gasoline on fiery coals, I soothed them with Water.

How Truthspeaking Heals

In Chapter 1, I told you that this was a healing book. Here in this chapter we have learned about some of the tools that make communication healing. Before we add more tools in the coming chapters, I would like to share a story of how, just as Water calms fiery coals, Truthspeaking can soothe us.

Addie was a new student in one of our year-long wilderness skills courses at the Teaching Drum Outdoor School. The culture shock of living in a close-knit group where it was impossible to practice her accustomed personal hygiene methods brought her face to face with one of her worst fears: being unclean and spreading her sexually transmitted disease. Past suicidal tendencies were beginning to surface, yet she couldn't bring herself to speaking her Truth with her campmates.

When I counseled with her, these were the reasons she gave for not speaking:

"It'll interfere with my education."

"I won't be accepted."

"I'll have to leave the group."

"I'll be lonely."

When I then asked what her Heart was telling her, she broke down. I knew the voice of her Heart, so she didn't have to verbalize it with me. Yet it was vital that she do so with her fellow students.

"Will you come with me for moral support?" she asked.

That afternoon we met with the rest of the students, and she spoke her Truth. She said it was a turning point in her life, as she was able to face her fears—all of them. For the first time, she could ground them in reality, which showed her which ones were illusions or projections and which ones were not. The newfound clarity allowed her to begin her healing on solid ground.

To live one's Truth is not to make a stand, but to stand up. It is not to be assertive, nor is it to sublimate, but to be fully who we are, fully present and engaged in the continuum of our lives. By claiming her Truth, Addie reclaimed her life. She discovered that Truth *is* life.

The more I speak my Truth, the more alive I am. This is because life exists only in the Now, and speaking my Truth is my expression of the Now. We who have figured out how to dwell in the past and the future merely exist. *Living in the past* and *living in the future* are oxymorons. The past is but a memory and the future is only a dream, so there is no life in either.

Even worse, dwelling in the past and future bleeds the life out of the Now. We rob ourselves of this precious gift of life that we are given only in this precious instant we call *the Now*. It is the only place where we can hope to encounter our Truth.

The Chapter at a Glance

The essence of Truth can be summed up as *direct*, *personal*, and *ever-changing*. An African saying tells us that Lion's story of the hunt will differ from Zebra's. Both were involved in the same hunt, yet because one was the hunter and the other was the hunted, each of their experiences was radically different. This is why Truth is not stated definitively. Instead terms like *maybe* and *if you wish* are either stated or implied by tone of voice and body language. This creates an opening for others to reflect upon what we share without feeling constrained by it.

Truth is fluid—a quality that points to its resilience, not its weakness. Because Truth is continually evolving, we need to communicate context along with fact. This helps listeners know us and why we came to our conclusions. At the same time it allows them to form their own conclusions.

Because Truth is ever changing, it is sometimes difficult to discern. Whenever I am in doubt about whether or not what I am about to say is my Truth, I ask myself: "Is it honoring, and does it foster relationship?" If my answer to both is "yes," I know I am speaking my Truth; and if my answer is "no," I look deeper to find my Truth.

The more I speak my truth, the more alive I am, because life exists only in the Now, and speaking my truth is my expression of the Now. We who have figured out how to dwell in the past and future merely exist. *Living in the past* and *living in the future* are oxymorons. The past is a memory and the future is only a dream, and there is no life in either. Both rob us of this precious gift of life that we are only given in this precious instant we call *the Now*, which is the bedrock of our Truth.

There are times when some of us cannot trust in the fact that speaking our Truth is all we need to do in order to express ourselves. We seek further validation by trying to get others to agree with our Truth. This is called *Stacking.*

When we feign respect in order to get our way, gain acceptance, or protect ourselves, we are *Fearspeaking*. We communicate only half-truths, which inevitably backfires. The use of "I" statements is a reliable indicator of honesty. The more "I" statements we use, the more honest we tend to be.

Our words and body language contain codes of either respect or disrespect. In the long run, how honorable and respectful we are with someone will mean more to him than whatever we may have talked about. Facts fade, but feelings linger.

When we choose not to speak our Truth, we have made the decision that our pride, fear, or assumptions are more important than the relationship. They dishonor an individual's Truth, deprive others of the experience of that Truth, and inevitably lead to conflict. When we resist this Fearspeaking, we cultivate a practice of Respect—first for ourselves, by acknowledging and embracing our Heartvoice; then for others, by speaking our Truth in the Now.

Chapter Three Endnotes

1 James Pennebaker, *The Secret Life of Pronouns: What Our Words Say About Us* (New York: Bloomsbury, 2011), 136.

2 James Pennebaker, *The Secret Life of Pronouns: What Our Words Say About Us*, 160.

3 John B. Pryor et al., "Self-Focused Attention and Self-Report Validity," *Journal of Personality* 45, no. 4 (1977): 526.

4 Merritt Ruhlen, *On the Origin of Languages: Studies in Linguistic Taxonomy,* (Stanford University Press, 1994), 271.

5 James Pennebaker, *The Secret Life of Pronouns: What Our Words Say About Us*, ix.

6 James Pennebaker, *The Secret Life of Pronouns: What Our Words Say About Us*, 200.

7 Wei Wu Wei, *Posthumous Pieces* (Hong Kong University Press, 1968), 55.

CHAPTER FOUR

WHAT TRUTH IS NOT

A cartoon strip popular with mental health professionals shows a person staring out at you from behind bars. In the second frame, you see that he is holding the bars up in front of him. The implication is that we create our own prison with our dysfunctional communication.

Think of Truth as breathing: if we do not exhale, we cannot inhale. We need to express our Truth in order to engage in the give-and-take of communication. When we do not voice our Truth, we create a communication boundary between self and other.

Take this common exchange:

"How are you?"

"I'm fine; how are you?"

The respondent did not speak her Truth, and she will probably not hear Truth in return. Here is another possible outcome:

"How are you?"

"I'm sad because I am not able to accept my son's anger, and the sadness has been hanging over me like a dark cloud all day. At the same time, I'm glad to see you! I came across this book I've been meaning to tell you about."

Here the respondent exhaled Truth, and she'll likely be able to inhale Truth in return. The reason is that she voiced what was in her Heart, rather than saying what she thought someone else would like to hear.

Some people look at the above example and mistake spontaneity—"I'm fine; how are you?"—for Truthspeaking. Sure, it is important to speak one's Truth in the Now; however, the emphasis is on *one's Truth* more than being reflexive. Seminole Medicine Man Sonny Billie says, "A knowledgeable Indian will often not say too much, and some white* folks might mistake this for being dumb. But we were taught not to speak too quickly unless we're sure of what we're saying because words can be like weapons, they can hurt."[1]

In the Civilized Way, we have grown accustomed to using words to hide the truth. The phrase *to speak with a forked tongue*—meaning to speak deceitfully or make false promises—is commonly used in reference to treaties made between the federal government and American Indian tribes. Yet even with the treaties, words in the form of language barriers, lies, and political maneuvering worked to the detriment of the tribes.[2]

The phrase is an allusion to serpents' tongues, which are scent organs. They are split, or "forked," to increase their efficiency.[3] However, because snakes are viewed as symbols of evil in Civilized culture, by extension the image of the forked tongue is also viewed as sinister.[4] Being split implies that words spoken by it are broken or insincere. We can speak one thing and mean another.

Truthspeaking, on the other hand, is rooted in the integrity and wholeness of the Circle Way. This means that we choose words to express ourselves sincerely and explicitly. In Chapter 5, we learn more about how to do this before speaking, and how to do it respectfully. First, though, we will explore the observations, beliefs, convictions, and forms of manipulative speech that we often falsely perceive as Truth. In doing so, we clear the path to our Heartvoice.

---

* The use of terms such as *white folk* and *white man* by Traditional Peoples is best understood today as symbolic references to what these terms represented—the Civilized Way—rather than literal references to either race or gender.

False Truths

Following are the seven most common forms of communication that we tend to confuse for Truth. I find that most people pretty easily recognize these false truths. Once we become aware of them, we tend to remember the uneasy feelings that typically accompany them.

1. Observations

What we perceive is central to our conception of the world and ourselves in it. Yet an observation alone is not Truth. In one of my wilderness immersion courses, one student loaned a Tomahawk to another, who returned it damaged. The loaner assumed the borrower had done it, and told him he could no longer use the tomahawk. It turned out that the borrower had returned the tomahawk undamaged, only to have someone else use it without permission.

The loaner's observation allowed him to construct a Faux Truth. Sharing his observation and opening it to examination allowed the Truth to be revealed.

My observation becomes Truth only when:

- **I share the observation** with all involved.
- **The observation is confirmed,** verbally or nonverbally, by all involved. *Without consensus confirmation, my observation remains just my observation.*

To effectively share an observation:

- **Be as a question**, which means to be open to any and all possibilities.
- **Ask permission** to share your observation.
- **Don't use the permission as an excuse to blame or externalize.** Honor the permission by sharing only what you observed.
- **Accept whatever transpires as Truth.**

HOW EXTERNALIZATIONS CREATE FALSE TRUTHS

The more we externalize, the more we isolate ourselves from our Truth. Only "I" statements keep me connected with my Heartvoice. "You did this," "You said that," etc. are interpretations and projections, oftentimes fueled by ego defensiveness or aggressiveness.

---

2. Facts and Beliefs

As already discussed, we often allow our observations to transform into facts, instead of questioning them to arrive more wholly at our Truth. It is said that seeing is believing; however, it is more accurate to say that believing is seeing. Perceiving is not an objective process, but a filtering process. We do not see, hear, or feel anything directly, but rather we construct it by running sensory input through beliefs and prior knowledge.

Similarly, many of us are of the opinion that because we are rational beings, Truth is arrived at by thinking. *Most often when we believe we are objectively thinking, we are only rearranging our preferences and prejudices.*

As a result, we commonly confuse facts for Truth, then proceed to make decisions based on them. Yet we often feel unsettled about those decisions, as facts come from outside ourselves, and they can be interpreted and reinterpreted. Truth, on the other hand, comes from the center of our being. It is not right or wrong, rational or irrational; it just *is*.

"The truth is more important than the facts,"[5] said architect Frank Lloyd Wright. In actuality, the two are often only coincidentally related, if at all. My wanting a new coat may or may not have anything to do with whether I need one, or whether it is cold outside. Truth stands on its own, with no need for support of any kind. If I am feeling lonely, I don't need to prove or justify it; and I can do something about it without fearing that my feeling might change.

A major Truthspeaking pitfall is allowing our observations to transform into (or reinforce) our beliefs. If I believe in ghosts,

I might see one outside my window instead of the Owl that is gliding by. My belief then becomes my Truth, even though it is a Faux Truth.

WHEN BELIEF BECOMES TRUTH

Belief takes on the illusion of Truth through the power of feeling, and through unshared, unquestioned observation. Many, if not most of us have an overriding belief that guides our lives. For some of us, this belief gives our life purpose and overall guidance. However, we risk deviating from our Truth when our beliefs become convictions.

---

3. Manipulative Speech

When we try to change a person or situation with chosen words, we are not speaking our Truth. At the same time, we are not being true to ourselves. Instead, we are being calculating and self-serving.

We may influence others when we speak our Truth in the moment, yet this does not qualify as being manipulative. Everything has its effect on something, and this includes our Truth.

Unless we twist our Truth to serve an end other than our Truth's pure expression, it is the responsibility of the listener to take our Truth at face value and not be unduly influenced by it.

4. Convictions

If my belief gets reinforcement from others, it could become a conviction—a belief spelled in capitals. It might become the rule of the universe or an overriding principle that makes everything wrong that falls outside its arch.

Many of us have a difficult time distinguishing conviction from Truth. Conviction arises when we:

- Embrace a belief
- Give this belief more credibility because others also embrace it.

- Decide to put our entire, unquestioning faith in it.

This process of belief transforming to conviction occurs because:

- We have not sought empirical evidence,
- We have lost our ability to be self-critical, and
- We have shut down to other points of view.

Embracing a belief as true for oneself is distinct from embracing one's personal Truth. Belief is founded upon unquestioned observation and serves a Faux Truth. This Faux Truth is exclusive to itself and has a high opinion of itself. This is why holders of Faux Truths tend to become elitist.

From psycho-emotional perspective, I note a very common three-step course that my clients take in evolving their convictions from Faux Truths:

1. **They feel alone.** Life is aimless. They need something to ease the endless pain.

2. **They need connection with other people**, and they have found an observation or idea that

   a. Makes them feel good,

   b. Unites them with others,

   c. Doesn't challenge them.,

3. **There is strength in numbers.** It goes from "How can all these people be wrong?" to "This is how we are going to live our lives—this is how we *should* live our lives," to "We will live and die for it!"

The birth of a conviction reveals a sense of desperation and a search for meaning. Yet the process is not intrinsic to the human experience. In the clan-based culture of our hunter-gatherer ancestors, everyone played vital roles in day-to-day existence. There was no need to give meaning to a life that was already steeped in purpose and direction.

Conviction appears to be purely a contemporary survival mechanism—an adaptive strategy to make some sense of a self-defeating life that denies our personal, ever-changing Truths and stifles their expression.

5. Oneness

At the core of Faux Truth is the mantra of Oneness—one top team, corporation, politician, truth, and so on, ad nauseam. This element of singularity leads us to struggle to have the last word, instead of listening and cherishing all voices.

To discern Truth, we must discard this concept of Oneness that underpins many of our observations, relationships, and convictions. Instead, we can embrace a spirit of Wholeness. The classic Zen poem *Hsin Hsin Ming*, or *Song of Trusting the Heart*, states:

In this world of the Beauty Way
There is neither self nor other.
To come immediately into balance with the way
When doubt arises just say "not two"
In this "not two," nothing is separate
There is nothing that is not included.[6]

When many of us hear "not two," we tend to think, "Well, that must mean one." I see this response as part of an entrapment hoop, which I call the *dichotomous perspective*: if it is not this it has to be that—either truth or untruth, black or white, self or other. We give ourselves no other choice.

Yet, as the last line of the stanza above states, this choice requires us to exclude everything else. I see it as the legacy of our isolation from nature. When we humans became sedentary agriculturalists, we formulated the original dichotomy: civilization or nature.

I see our concept of Oneness as purely an illusion. I don't witness it in the natural world: no ant is a colony, no tree is a forest. The Native Elders I have learned from refer to the Circle Way, where everything is included; and to the Web of Life, where everything is connected. The Elders talk of Wholeness and integrity, rather than Oneness and singularity.

Behind city walls, Oneness is a necessity for survival. It is the fuel that keeps the walls standing by creating an *us-civilized* and *them-wild* dichotomy. Outside city gates and pasture fences, though, oneness is a word without meaning—because there is nothing that is not included in the Web of Life.

6. The Right-and-Wrong Trap

The idea of Wholeness applies to Truthspeaking as well. One person's perception is another's person's deception. In other words, one person's Truth is not the next person's. If someone tries to make someone else's Truth hers, it will lead her astray, isolating her from both herself and her organic connection with her world.

My Truth does not make your Truth a lie. That would be like taking one part of something and calling it the whole. We each contribute to the greater Truth with our personal Truths. Though one person's Truth runs contrary to another's, just like night and day seem to be opposites, they are actually mates, essential to each other and together comprising the whole.

In a healthy relationship, with Truthspeaking at its core, there is no right or wrong. Each person holds and speaks his own truth, takes personal responsibility for his words and actions, and embraces the truth of the other, no matter what it is. When we do this, we create a supportive environment for acceptance, understanding, and healing.

When we tell someone else he is wrong:

- We are either not hearing or accepting his Truth, or
- We are judging, externalizing, or defending.
- Our position reflexively becomes right or elevated, which means
- We don't have to take blame or responsibility.

When we consider ourselves wrong:

- We are not respecting our own Truth.
- We take the power away from our Heartvoice and surrender it to someone else.

- We take blame or responsibility for someone, which enables him to evade his Truth, and

- We disable him from taking personal responsibility for his actions.

By embracing our Truth *and* his Truth, we transcend the either-or confines of *right and wrong*. We deepen our sense of Wholeness by sharing our Truths.

SHARING TRUTH IS VITAL

Our Truth is not something to keep for ourselves, as it quickly goes rancid when it is not expressed in the moment. It is as though we turn on a flashlight and stick it in a drawer. The batteries are slowly sapped of their energy, and the light dims and dims until it goes out. The same thing happens with our vital energy: we grow less and less emotionally expressive and we become less and less sensitive to the feelings of others. People start avoiding us, and we risk sinking into the darkness of depression.

---

7. *Advice, Mediation, and Arbitration*

"Is giving advice, Truthspeaking?" a client once asked me.

I replied that my experience with advice-giving is that it is usually one person's effort to project his or her Truth upon another. If we were to truly help another person, we would be encouraging her to get in touch with her own Truth—her own source of advice. Giving advice tends to short-circuit this process of finding one's own Truth. This happens either because of our influence or in reaction to it.

If advice-giving is often not welcome and usually not helpful, why do we do it?

When I ask this question of my clients, their answers fall into three categories:

1. **The desire to feel superior** (usually because of low self-esteem).

2. **The need to feel accepted.**

3. An effort to control.

When people start working on these core motivating factors for advice-giving, they usually find that their desire to give advice wanes.

"What is your opinion on mediation and arbitration being Truthspeaking tools?" a therapist once asked me.

"I think they can serve well in bringing the involved parties to a place of mutual understanding, and perhaps to a point of working relationship," I replied. "Yet these tools are not Truthspeaking, nor do they address Truthspeaking."

"They help primarily with surface patterns," I continued, "and to focus on workable solutions. Truth dwells below that. In fact, not being in touch with the underlying Truth—and honoring it—causes the conflict and resulting need for mediation and arbitration."

"Mediation can be a drawn-out, verbose process," I concluded, "and it usually results in a compromise of some sort. On the other hand, the underlying Truths could be expressed in short order, with much less need for compromise."

IS CRITICISM TRUTHSPEAKING?

Some people think so. They say that it's good to get it off of your chest: to tell someone straight up what you think about him. Unless an individual requests constructive criticism, nearly all critiquing is essentially externalizing: statements on how you do not match up to my perceptions, beliefs, or expectations. In essence I am judging your performance or character. No matter what the guise, criticism is diametrically opposed to Truthspeaking. This doesn't mean that Truthspeaking is all about appeasement. In reality, Truthspeaking creates a context in which people feel safe, inspired, and loved enough to change and grow.

When Speech Becomes Manipulation

At one time or another, nearly all of us have spoken to backhandedly influence or express something, rather than directly voicing our Truths. We can do it by simply using *but* in a sentence. For some of us, manipulative speech has become an unconscious habit. Others—especially those who feel victimized or disenfranchised—often resort to this form of speech, as do many with mercenary and other exploitative motivations.

Expressing a hidden agenda often appears to be safer and more effective than directly expressing our thoughts and feelings. This encourages us to continue with it and refine it. However, everything has its price. The more we speak words which are not our truth, the more disconnected we become from ourselves, and the more disenchanted we become with life.

Meeting our self-expressive needs underhandedly leads to dysfunctional and short-lasting relationships. Yet some of us know of no other way to express ourselves, so we hop on the endless treadmill of feint and manipulation—which keeps us draining and discarding relationships.

It takes real diligence to change manipulative speech patterns. Fortunately, the approach is simple, which gives us more than a fighting chance. Here are the steps I recommend for meeting expressive needs in a way that is both respectful and helps create healthy relationship:

- Before you speak, ask yourself, "What am I trying to get?"
- If you identify something hidden, refrain from speaking and go to the next step.
- Identify the hidden need.
- Follow the need down to the core feeling from which it arose (see Chapter 10).
- Express your core feeling, as this is your Truth.

Trust that change is possible. Direct speech comes naturally; we just have to create an opening for it. If we can take Step 1 above, there is a good chance that we will be able to follow through with the rest of the steps. The mere fact that we are asking the question shows that we are ready. And capable.

For a few of us, though, the pattern of manipulative speech is going to be much harder than that to break. When this is the case, I suggest seeking competent professional help.

Following are the two most common forms of manipulative speech. Recognizing them, and how we use them, is a big help in recognizing what we are trying to get (Step 1 above).

What "But" Says

"I love you, but I can't live with you."

"I want to go, but I have work to do."

"My heart says yes, but my head says no."

In none of these cases is the person speaking her Truth. This is so with virtually all *but* statements. At best, she can only be speaking a shade of her Truth, as there is no contradiction in the Voice of Heart.

But creates the contradiction. Whatever follows a *but* severely limits or alters what precedes it, if not outright negating it. Imagine what "I love you" would mean to you if it were followed by "I can't live with you." *Each of our Truths needs to be honored by having it stand alone, instead of making it compete with another Truth.*

Backhanded Comments

These are externalizations of unmet needs. We usually resort to them when we feel unheard, yet we do not feel empowered enough to share this Truth. Instead, we deliver an emotionally charged or blaming comment under our breaths, often after a discussion is over. It is a feeble appeal to Oneness and a desperate effort to have the last word.

Feeling the urge to utter a backhanded comment is our clue to look for the underlying feeling. By expressing this feeling, we speak our personal Truths, rather than using our words insincerely, and as weapons.

Responding to backhanded comments often triggers a battle of egos. Instead, we can create space for the person to express her Truth by gently asking what she needs or what she is feeling.

The Chapter at a Glance

As we clear a path to our Heartvoice, we will unpack some of the things we often falsely perceive as Truth: observations, convictions, and other forms of manipulative speech.

Observations are central to our perception of the world and ourselves in it—but an observation only becomes Truth when I share it with all involved, and when the observation is then verbally or nonverbally confirmed by them. To effectively share an observation, begin by remaining open to all possibilities; then, ask permission to share your observation, and honor that permission by sharing only what you observed.

We often allow our observations to transform into facts or beliefs, instead of questioning them to arrive more wholly at our Truth. Many of us are of the opinion that because we are rational beings, Truth is arrived at by thinking. Most often when we believe we are objectively thinking, we are only rearranging our preferences and prejudices. It is said that seeing is believing; however, it is more accurate to say that believing is seeing. If I believe in ghosts, I might see one outside my window instead of the Owl gliding by.

When my belief gets reinforcement from others, it could become a conviction—an overriding truth that makes everything else wrong. Beliefs and convictions are founded upon unquestioned observation; they lack empirical evidence, critiquing, and openness to other points of view.

When we use a *but* in our speech, we create a contradiction that severely limits, alters, or negates what precedes it. We undermine our Truth, because there is no contradiction in the voice of the Heart. When we resort to backhanded comments, we abuse our words by using them as weapons.

These false Truths reveal a sense of desperation and a search for meaning in a culture that stifles the expression of Truth. In the clan-based cultures of our hunter-gatherer ancestors, where everyone played vital roles in day-to-day existence, there was no need to give meaning to a life that was already steeped in purpose and direction.

The more we speak words which are not our Truths, the more disconnected we become from our self and the more disenchanted we become with life. We rely all the more on observations, beliefs, convictions, and other forms of manipulative speech. We adopt the mantra of Oneness: one top team, corporation, or leader. This drives us to have the last word, instead of listening and cherishing all voices.

The Native Elders I apprenticed to refer to the Circle Way, where everything is honored and included; and to the Web of Life, where everything is connected. They emphasize wholeness and integral relationship, rather than Oneness and singularity.

My Truth does not make your Truth a lie. That would be like taking one part of something and calling it the whole. We each contribute to the greater Truth by sharing our personal Truths. Though one person's Truth runs contrary to another's, just like night and day seem to be opposites, they are actually mates, essential to each other and together comprising the whole.

Chapter Four Endnotes

1   Shirley Ann Jones, *Simply Living: The Spirit of the Indigenous People* (Canada: New World Library, 1999), 150.

2   Wade Davies, *American Indian Sovereignty and Law: An Annotated Bibliography*, (Scarecrow Press, 2009), 36-49.

3   Kurt Schwenk, "Why Snakes Have Forked Tongues," *Science* 263, no. 5153 (1994): 1573-1577.

4   Ibid.

5   Frank Lloyd Wright, *Frank Lloyd Wright: Letters to Architects*, (California State University Press, 1984), 170.

6   Tamarack Song, *Song of Trusting the Heart: A Classic Zen Poem for Daily Meditation*, (Sentient Publications, 2011), 24.

CHAPTER FIVE

TO KNOW YOUR HEART IS TO KNOW TRUTH

Through no fault of our own, we lead largely unauthentic lives. As well-intended and sincere as we might want to be, we each lie on average three times during a ten-minute conversation.[1] And how many times a day do we simply refrain from speaking our thoughts and feelings? Why is it that we do not just speak from our Hearts? Do humans have a naturally malevolent or deceptive character trait?

I think it is actually the opposite. My study of aboriginal cultures around the world shows us to be creatures of spontaneous and authentic expressiveness when we are living in our natural state.

So, what happened that caused whole institutions and industries to dedicate themselves to finding ways of convincing the populace that illusion is truth—that it is better *not* to speak from our Hearts? In 1952, why did the War Department start calling itself the Defense Department? In 1954, why did General Mills create the fictitious motherly figure Betty Crocker and create a line of instant cake mixes in her name? And when they flopped, why did the company hire Freudian psychotherapists to determine that women were not buying the mixes because they felt guilty?

The women thought they were not providing for their families if they didn't put some effort into making a cake. The analysts recommended that the women be asked to add an egg to the mix. General Mills went on to make millions of dollars on their cake mixes.

What does government and corporate spin have to do with knowing our Hearts and expressing our Truth? We are the products of our culture—we cannot help but reflect its mores. At the same time, we are intrinsically creatures of integrity: we want to be authentic. We need to trust and be trusted. As insecure and unsure of ourselves as we might be, we still take pains to sound as though we are speaking from our Hearts. In fact, we are so successful that we often convince ourselves that we are doing so.

The Return to Heart

In the previous chapter, I included an excerpt from *Song of Trusting the Heart*. I would now like to return to that poem, because poetry is the voice of the Heart and speaks easily to it. When we hear poetry, we must listen to it from the Heart. This is expressed in the following lines:

> The Beauty Way is not difficult
> For those who have no preferences
> *However, make the least distinction...*
> *When we hold onto a thought, the truth is hidden.*
> *Things become confusing and wrong.*
> *To seek Heart with the mind*
> *Is the greatest of all mistakes.*
> *To the Heart there is no duality*

The mind creates confusion, and that's its job. All things are one in the Web of Life, yet the mind is designed to tear the Web apart. How else would I know which is the ripest apple to pick, or which words to choose for sharing these thoughts with you? Confusion, then, is a gift. It is not life itself, but it is the way by which I navigate life.

However, it is not the *only* way to navigate life. My Ojibwe Elders talk of the *Giizis Miikana*, or *Sun Trail*, which is the Path of Life. We are all connected with the Giizis Miikana through our Hearts. When we listen to our Heart voices, it is the voice of the Giizis Miikana. Here is how we reassemble the Web that the mind has shredded; here is where all comes together as one, life is clear, and relationships are straightforward. The Elders told me that to arrive at this place, our minds must serve our Hearts, rather than the other way around.

When I go to my mind, the one become many; and when I return to my Heart, the many again become one. The problem, as *Song of Trusting the Heart* states, arises *When we hold on to a thought...[then] things become confusing and wrong.*

IS IT HEART OR MIND VOICE?

Here are ways to tell:

- *The Heart needs no time to come to clarity, and the mind belabors issues.*
- *The voice of the mind is accompanied by at least the faint shadow of doubt.*
- *When the Heart speaks, the mind sometimes follows up by saying, "Not so loud!"*

Living in balance, the Elders explained to me, is dwelling in the Heart. This does not mean that we reject the mind. Rather we are to always return to the Heart. The mind and the Heart do not have to be in competition; like night and day, they are designed to complement each other. The Heart tells us what to do and the head tells us how to do it.

I saw the opposite of this principle played out during a couples counseling session, when one of them stated, "My partner and I just spent two days working out a conflict between us."

"Whenever it takes a lengthy amount of time to work something out," I replied, "it's usually because it is being approached from the ego, which means head-based rather than Heart-based communication. It might seem at first as though you have resolved something; however, seldom does anything really get settled in this way. Sooner or later it resurfaces, and it can come back again and again. The despair and frustration grows."

They both nodded in agreement, then acknowledged the fact that this was hardly the first time they had tried to hammer through an issue.

"Truthspeaking is connecting from the Heart," I continued. "It is much quicker, more satisfying, and lasting than banging heads together."

NATIVE WISDOM

Many traditional cultures emphasize the Heart over the mind in their language and in their practices:

- *The Ojibwe word for Heart is ode, and the word for village is odana, which means place of many Hearts.*
- *In 1891, Oglala Lakota chief Four Guns said, "To the Indian, words that are true sink deep into his Heart, where they remain in silence; he never forgets them."[2]*
- *Wandiuk Marika, an Elder Australian Aborigine, would say, "I'm not just talking from just the talk, I'm talking from my Heart, deep from my Heart."[3]*
- *"[While I was an adolescent learning from the Elders] my world had become much bigger than I had ever dreamed. I had learned to see things with my Heart, not just the body 'eye.'"[4]— Hawaiian Elder Kaili'ohe Kame'ekua*
- *There is a Congolese saying, The teeth are smiling, but is the Heart?*
- *I learned many English words...could recite some of the Ten Commandments... I knew how to sleep in a bed, pray to Jesus, comb my hair, use a toilet, [and] I learned that a person thinks with his head instead of his Heart." – Hopi Elder Sun Chief[5]*
- *Krishnamurti described the inner fragmentation as, "You think one thing, say something else, then do something else entirely different."[6]*

That we must *return* to the Heart means that some degree of separation exists between it and our thoughts. Michael Koenigs of the Department of Psychiatry at the University of Wisconsin-Madison, suggests that because humans weigh emotional and rational perspectives against one another when making a decision, distinct neurological systems are involved in the process. Although both are part of a single, larger neural system, they manifest as competing decision-making processes.[7]

Why do we need to return to our Hearts? Renowned physicist David Bohm said that, as things currently stand, we don't control our thoughts—our thoughts control us. They separate us from nature, they put us at odds with other people—and with ourselves—and they dump more and more out-of-control situations into our laps. Our minds then tell us that this is all a good thing: simply part of life as rational beings. In a BBC interview, Carl Jung said, "We need more understanding of human nature, because the only real danger that exists is man himself... And we are pitifully unaware of it. We know nothing of man... far too little. His psyche should be studied—because we are the origin of all coming evil."[8]

These psychic epidemics emerge when we dwell in our thoughts instead of our Hearts. Ours is a scarcity-based culture: we are conditioned to be unsatisfied, unfulfilled, and mistrusting. Instead of speaking from our Hearts, where we can embrace life as both whole and full, we have been conditioned to speak from the mind. Yet, when we speak from our minds, most if not all of our communication is essentially an expression of need, or a defense of need. Contentment comes only from what we have, and of course we never have enough, as we are bombarded with the constant message to acquire and achieve more and more and more. The quantity doesn't matter; it is by embracing the mind first that we keep feeding this construct of need.

A Native person generally approaches situations from her Heart-of-Hearts: that place where feeling, intellect, intuition, senses, and ancestral memories meet. When we look at a situation from only one of these, we rely on a narrow perspective. As a result, we have a grasp that leaves us able to see very few, if any, options.

Instead, a Native makes a multi-dimensional decision that balances many perceptions, while at the same time broadening her own.

Often, when the members of a group each come from their Heart-of-Hearts, the shared awareness that results shows that the presumed problem wasn't so drastic after all. Listening and empathy alone often resolve the situation. If not, all the rich perspectives flow together to provide workable solutions that tend to speak to everybody.

Truth and Morality

When we tame our thoughts, we relax our egos and give ourselves the opportunity to open our Hearts. We thus return to the seat of our morality, which here means the capacity for empathy and altruism—the deeper forms of human connection. As expressed by the Sufi poet Rumi:

> *They say there is a window from one Heart to another. How can there be a window where no wall remains?*[9]

Morality is not a learned behavior, but rather a biological function that is hardwired in our brains. With no preconditioning, young children make decisions informed by moral considerations.[10] They exhibit moral behaviors and emotions (such as understanding the difference between a truth and a lie) even if they may not have a concrete sense of themselves as moral individuals.[11]

WE ARE NOT ALONE

A number of other animals (thus far Dolphins,[12] Great Apes,[13] Elephants,[14] and Magpies[15]) have been found with moral capacities and the ability exhibit moral characteristics.[16]

Unfortunately, much can inhibit our proclivity to speak and act from our moral consciousness. Emotional and hormonal influences, along with cultural conditioning and learned dysfunctional behavioral patterns, work to distort or censor our ethical voice.[17] When we connect with our Heartvoice, we can override much of what masks our moral sensitivity.

We return to the Heart because it is our natural center. It is only in the Civilized Way that we have embraced the belief that the mind is our base. Vernon Harper, a Northern Cree from Canada, puts it this way: "Some people say that animals are ignorant, but in many ways they're really smarter than us. You don't see a dog trying to be an eagle. You don't see a squirrel trying to be a wolf....Plants and animals follow their instructions. It's the human beings who don't follow theirs."[31]

Truthspeaking is Heart-to-Heart communication—intrinsic human communication. There can be no lies when we speak from our Heart-of-Hearts, because our Heartvoice is our personal Truth. What we say and what we hear is all Truth.

As we conclude Part I of this book and begin Part II by examining the Art of Listening, I will leave you with these words, spoken by Como, a Potawatomi Chief: "I'm opening my Heart to speak to you...open yours to receive my words."[18]

The Chapter at a Glance

To become Truthspeakers, we must challenge the way of civilized culture relying solely on the mind. Instead, as my Ojibwe Elders explained to me, we must dwell in the Heart in order to live in balance. That doesn't mean we reject the mind, only that we remember to always return to the Heart. They don't have to be in competition with each other, as they are as complementary as night and day. The Heart tells us what to do and the head tells us how to do it.

My Elders have told me that the Giizis Miikana (Ojibwe for the *Sun Trail*) is the Path of Life, and that we are connected with it through our Hearts. When we listen to our heartvoice, it is the voice of the Giizis Miikana, the voice of Life. Here the Elders say, all come together as one, life is clear, and relationships are straightforward. To arrive at this clarity, the mind must serve the Heart, not the other way around.

Renowned physicist David Bohm says that as things currently stand, we don't control our thoughts—our thoughts control us. They separate us from nature, they put us at odds with other people, they put us at odds with ourselves, and they dump more and more out-of-control situations into our laps. Then our minds tell us that this is all a good thing, simply part of life as rational beings.[19] In a BBC interview, Carl Jung said, "We need more understanding of human nature, because the only real danger that exists is man himself... And we are pitifully unaware of it. We know nothing of man... far too little. His psyche should be studied—because we are the origin of all coming evil."[20]

When we tame our thoughts, we relax our egos and give ourselves the opportunity to open our Hearts. This allows us to return to the seat of our morality, which here means the capacity for empathy and altruism.

Morality is not a learned behavior, but rather a biological function that is hardwired in our brains.[21] With no preconditioning, young children incorporate moral considerations into their decision-making processes.[22]

A number of other animals, such as Dolphins,[23] Great Apes,[24] Elephants,[25] and Magpies,[26] have been found to exhibit moral characteristics.[27]

Much can get in the way of speaking and acting from our moral consciousness. Emotional and hormonal influences, cultural conditioning, and learned dysfunctional behavioral patterns work to distort or censor our moral voice.[28] When we connect with our Heartvoice, we can override much of what masks the ethical component of our Heart-of-Hearts.

When we return to the Heart and dwell in it, we engage in the authentically human communication that is Truthspeaking— we begin to live by these words of Potawatomi Chief Como: "I'm opening my Heart to speak to you...open yours to receive my words." I would only ask you to consider the same as we conclude Part I of this book and begin Part II by examining the Art of Listening.

Chapter Five Endnotes

1   Robert S. Feldman, James A. Forrest, and Benjamin R. Happ, "Self-Presentation and Verbal Deception: Do Self-Presenters Lie More?" *Basic and Applied Social Psychology* 24 (2002): 170.

2   Virginia Irving Armstrong, *I Have Spoken* (Chicago: The Swallow Press, 1971), 131.

3   Wandjuk Marika and Jennifer Isaacs, *Wandjuk Marika: Life Story* (University of Queensland Press, 1995), 18.

4   Pali Lee and Koko Willis, *Tales from the Night Rainbow* (Night Rainbow, 1988), 46.

5   Don C. Talayesva, *Sun Chief: The Autobiography of a Hopi Indian* (Yale University Press, 1945), 99.

6   Krishnamurti, *Think on These Things* (HarperOne, 1989), 121.

7   Liane Young and Michael Koenigs, "Investigating Emotion in Moral Cognition: A Review of Evidence from Functional Neuroimaging and Neuropsychology." *British Medical Bulletin* 84, no. 1 (2007): 69-79.

8   C.G. Jung, interview by John Freeman, "Face to Face," *C.G. Jung Speaking: Interviews and Encounters*, BBC (October 1959).

9   Rumi, *Thief of Sleep: 180 Quatrains from the Persian*, trans. Shahram Shiva (Prescott, AZ: Hohm Press, 2000), 24.

10 Jason M. Cowell and Jean Decety, "The Neuroscience of Implicit Moral Evaluation and its Relation to Generosity in Early Childhood," *Current Biology* 25, no. 1 (2015): 93-97.

11 Tobias Krettenauer, Samantha Campbell and Steven Hertz, "Moral Emotions and the Development of the Moral Self in Childhood." *European Journal of Developmental Psychology* 10, no. 2 (2013): 159-173.

12 D. Reiss and L. Marino, "Mirror Self-Recognition in the Bottlenose Dolphin: A Case of Cognitive Convergence," *Proc. National Academy of Sciences U.S.A.* 98, no. 10 (2001): 5937-42.

13 G.G. Gallop Jr., "Chimpanzees: Self-Recognition," *Science* 167, no. 3914 (1970): 86-7.

14 J.M. Plotnik et al., "Self-Recognition in an Asian Elephant," *Proc. National Academy of Sciences U.S.A.* 103, no. 45 (2006): 17053-7.

15 H. Prior et al., "Mirror-Induced Behavior in the Magpie (Pica Pica): Evidence of Self-Recognition," *PloS Biology* 6, no. 8 (2008): e202.

16 Philip Hunter, "The basis of morality," *EMBO Reports* 11, no. 3 (2010): 166-9.

17 Manuel Fumagalli and Alberto Priori, "Functional and Clinical Neuroanatomy of Morality," *Brain* 135, no. 7 (2012): 2006-21.

18 Thomas Jefferson and Henry Augustine Washington, *The Writings of Thomas Jefferson* (J.C. Riker, 1854), 180.

19 David Bohm, *Thought as a System* (Routledge, 1994), 45.

20 C.G. Jung, interview by John Freeman, "Face to Face," *C.G. Jung Speaking: Interviews and Encounters*, BBC (October 1959).

21 J. Kiley Hamlin, "The Infantile Origins of Our Moral Brains," in *The Moral Brain: A Multidisciplinary Perspective* (The MIT Press, 2015), 105-23.

22 Gavin Nobes, Georgia Panagiotaki, and Kimberley J. Bartholomew, "The Influence of Intention, Outcome and Question-Wording on Children's and Adults' Moral Judgments," *Cognition* 157 (2016): 190, DOI: 10.1016/j.cognition.2016.08.019.

23 D. Reiss and L. Marino, "Mirror Self-Recognition in the Bottlenose Dolphin: A Case of Cognitive Convergence," 5937-42.

24 G.G. Gallop Jr., "Chimpanzees: Self-Recognition," 86-7.

25 J.M. Plotnik et al., "Self-Recognition in an Asian Elephant," 17053-7.

26 H. Prior et al., "Mirror-Induced Behavior in the Magpie (Pica Pica): Evidence of Self-Recognition," e202.

27 Philip Hunter, "The Basis of Morality," *EMBO Rep.* 11, no. 3 (2010): 166-9.

28 Manuel Fumagalli and Alberto Priori, "Functional and Clinical Neuroanatomy of Morality," *Brain* 135 (2012): 2006-21.

≈≈≈

PART TWO

THE ART OF LISTENING

When we truly listen, we accept what we hear as though we already know it. If this sounds strange, it is only because we have lost touch with the fact that relationship is Heart-centered. Instead, we have learned to connect with each other through the mind. As we progress through the following four chapters, we will see how there can be no Truthspeaking without listening from the Heart, and how listening can be even more relationship-engaging than speaking.

Traditional Hawaiians stress the importance of listening when they say *He lohe ke ola, he kuli ka make[1]*—To hear is life, to turn a deaf ear is death. We can speak our Truths until we are blue in the face, but if nobody listens—if nobody knows *how* to listen—we might as well save our breaths, as nothing in effect was spoken. Every voice needs an open and accepting ear to receive it, and these next pages will guide us to that place.

CHAPTER SIX

LISTENING FROM THE HEART

The ability to speak my Truth is based entirely upon my ability to listen—and not just to others. If I can't hear my Truth, I cannot voice it; and if I am not able to hear the Truth of another, I cannot honor it. The term *Truthspeaking* is to some degree a misnomer, as listening is the fundamental element.

The Ojibwe people in my area have a term, *bizindam*, which ostensibly means *listen*. At the same time, it means *Truth*. When we listen with our Heart, we hear the Truth in all things. Another Ojibwe term, *debwewin*, is typically translated as *Truth*. Yet to fully understand the concept of debwewin, we must realize that it also means *listen*, for there is no Truth without listening.

Henry David Thoreau said, "It takes two to speak the truth— one to speak and another to hear." Truthspeaking and Truthlistening are like our right and left legs; each is equally important, as without either one we would be severely imbalanced. Infants, who learn to speak by first listening, are a prime example for us.

There are times when we speak little or not at all, yet we listen all the time. In our culture, much is said of taking personal responsibility for what we say. I suggest that we also take responsibility for how we listen.

We tend to think of listening as a mechanical process: we close our mouths and open our ears. Listening is actually a skill of the highest order. In this chapter, we learn how to bear witness to Truth by becoming better listeners.

Right away we hit a snag, because we are accustomed to stating our case and arguing it. When what we speak is embraced, we feel fulfilled; and when it is not, we immediately work on how best to rephrase it, then wait for the next chance to speak and to win. Yet is this really winning—and when do we listen?

When we promote our positions, we are only repeating what we already know, which is limited to our experience and ability. If our position prevails, everybody is limited to our experience and ability.

Listening is a more effective way of being heard than speaking. When we listen respectfully and attentively, we create an environment for being heard. Other people give us perspective, and they give us reflections of ourselves. When everybody listens to each other, everyone is heard—including us. We have created a win-win situation: each person's perspective is incorporated, and the whole benefits from each individual's contribution.

When we prioritize listening, we speak far more powerfully than if our focus were on speaking alone. This is a manifestation of what many Native peoples mean when they say *Giving is receiving*. It is what the Ojibwe mean when they say *Truth is listening* and *Listening is Truth*.

Have Big Ears

"I was out in this clearing gathering greens," said my long-time assistant, Abel, "when I looked up into the eyes of a Deer. She was about thirty paces away, doing the same thing as me—gathering greens. I didn't want to startle her, so I went right back to picking. She flicked her tail, showing she was a little nervous; but then she went back to browsing. Out of the corner of my eye, I noticed that she'd look my way every once in a while, but I didn't pay her any mind, and we did well together."

I told Abel about how Wolves can wander in amongst a herd of Caribou, who will remain calm—as long as the Wolves aren't hungry. The Caribou can tell the difference; and the Wolves, being Truthspeakers, don't try to deceive the Caribou. If the Wolves did, it would be to their detriment, because the Caribou would no longer let the Wolves anywhere near them.

When the Wolves are hungry, they stealthily stalk up as close as they can to the Caribou, then break into a final rush. The startled Caribou bolt away; and any old, weak, or lame stand out like sore thumbs. The Wolves instinctively key in on the weakest one, and they all cooperate to bring her down.

This way of hunting keeps both Wolf and Caribou sharp and healthy. It develops trust between them: each knows what the other is up to and why.

After a while," Abel went on to say, "a family of three Gray Jays came into the clearing. One sailed by me and raised a ruckus. [In the Hoop of Relations, Jays perform the role of sentry, and everyone trusts in their alarms.] The Deer's tail went up, she snorted, and she bolted away."

Did she have to? Perhaps not, as she knew Abel was no threat. The Jays, however, were thinking beyond the Deer, and beyond themselves. That Deer couldn't be sure why the Jays were calling the alarm, yet she knew to trust in it. False alarm or not, she couldn't take the chance to ignore it.

She often never finds out why the alarm was raised, yet her trust in Jay never wanes. This is a survival trait that is imprinted in her genetic memory. Those who doubted were eliminated from the gene pool long ago.

In this story, we see how important it is to listen to—and trust in—not just what we hear, but what lies beyond it. Like the wild animals, we are each like an organ within an organism, performing a separate and valuable function—when we get outside of ourselves and trust in other voices.

The animals must listen as well to the silence, which often precedes a predator attack. We can do the same, as the silence between words is a vital part of the conversation.

Truthlistening Begins with Silence

Theater critic John Lahr says, "Accustomed to the veneer of noise...society is suspicious of those who value silence."[2] Being a verbally oriented people, we tend to view silence as merely the absence of speech. For many of us, silence is to be avoided at all cost.

For some traditional peoples, silence creates a sense of presence that says more than words. The act of sitting in silence with someone creates trust and rapport. It is a tangible sign of interest and commitment. When words are finally spoken, they are more likely clear Truth, as opposed to initial words that would otherwise be thrown out to see if there is trust and rapport.

Ohiyesa, the Santee Dakota we heard from earlier in the book, tells us what silence represents for the individual: "We believe profoundly in silence—the sign of a perfect equilibrium. Silence is the absolute poise or balance of body, mind, and spirit. Those who can preserve their selfhood ever calm and unshaken by the storms of existence—not a leaf, as it were, astir on the tree; not a ripple upon the shining pool—those, in the mind of the person of nature, possess the ideal attitude and conduct of life."[3]

Ote Kte (Plenty Kill), a contemporary of Ohiyesa's and a chief of the Oglala Lakota, elaborates on what silence represents for others: "Silence was meaningful with the Lakota, and this granting a space of silence before talking was done in the practice of true politeness and regardful of the rule that *thought comes before speech*." He went on: "And in the midst of sorrow, sickness, death, or misfortune of any kind, and in the presence of the notable and great, silence was the mark of respect. More powerful than words was silence with the Lakota...The silent man was ever to be trusted, while the man ever ready with speech was never taken seriously."[4]

Here is another value to silence, expressed by Haunani-Kay Trask, a Native Hawaiian woman: "To know my history... I had to begin to speak my language with our Elders and leave long silences for wisdom to grow."[5]

A wise old owl sat on an oak
The more he saw, the less he spoke
The less he spoke, the more he heard
Why aren't we like that wise old bird?
– By Edward H. Richards[6]

The Reasons for Silence

First: we honor another's Truth by listening to it in silence.

We do the reverse by using silence mainly as a pause in our own speech. As M. Scott Peck, author of *The Road Less Traveled*, said, "An essential part of true listening is...the temporary giving up or setting aside of one's own prejudices, frames of reference and desires so as to experience as far as possible the speaker's world from the inside, step in inside his or her shoes."

Second: listening in silence is being as a question.

We become more conscious of what we sense and intuit. We are much better designed for receiving than transmitting: our five senses (taste, touch, sight, hearing, and smell) are all devoted to gathering information. Their range and strength are much greater than our range of transmission.

Third: being silent offers an invitation for others to speak from the Heart.

Conscious silence creates an empty bowl, which gives space for another person's Truth, opens us to possibilities, and readies us to receive whatever comes. This means listening without debate, reaction, or judgment, as each of them is a form of shutting down, creating a wall, or denying another's Truth.

Fourth: silence helps us listen beyond the voice of the speaker.

Where does the voice come from? What is it crying out that is voiceless? What Truths are the words masking? Silence is vital to answering these questions. Musical notes would be little more than a jumble of noise were it not for the silences between them that structure the melody and give pulse to the rhythm.

WHERE IS SILENCE?

Recently someone asked if I thought a weekly day of silence could be a stepping-stone to Truthlistening. "It could give a feel for what gifts silence can bring," I replied. "Yet much more is needed, like learning to honor the silence in every day and moment, in order to be continually open to the Truth around us. We want to learn how to enter silence when it will most encourage another to speak his Truth. It takes everyday practice to develop this sensitivity and spontaneity. More than a place to go or something to carve out, silence is an inner calm and receptiveness."

Silent Communication

It is said that we have two ears for stereoscopic hearing. Yet we have only one mouth. This is so that we can listen more than talk. Think of using one ear to listen to a speaker's words, and the other to attune to her nonverbal presence. As Ohiyesa said, "It should be remembered that among Indians the whole body speaks."[7]

When we hear somebody speak, we naturally key in on the silences before, between and after the words. Polish poet Stanislaw J. Lec says, *There are grammatical errors even in...silence.*[8] Anticipation, feeling, and reaction are contained in the pauses rather than the words. The setting, facial expressions, body language, relationship to the speaker, history with the subject matter, and so much more, flesh out the bare words.

Intrinsic to communication, body language is used to focus attention and express intent, emotion, and thought. Body language serves as both stand-alone communication and a partner to verbal communication. Social anthropologist Edward T. Hall says that up to sixty percent of what we communicate is nonverbal.[9] Body language, which includes facial expressions, gestures, and posturings of the arms, legs, head, and torso, often conveys meaning more precisely than words.

Remember that the nonverbal component can be either supportive or detracting. We can convey that we are going to be fully present, without expectation or interruption. Or we can show that we are primarily waiting for our turn to speak. Our silence speaks on many levels, and the speaker will likely intuit all that it says.

I Speak, You Listen

Sometimes people who engage in dialogue lose sight of the listening component. In effect, we are looking for an audience for our monologues. We often interrupt those who are speaking, or we have to bite our tongues until we find a break to speak. We typically do it for these reasons:

- We feel insecure in the situation.
- We struggle with low self-esteem.
- We have little regard for the speaker.
- We are reactive or critical.
- We want to enable, rescue, or judge the speaker.

TIP TO AVOID INTERRUPTING

No matter the reason, we dishonor the speaker and his Truth when we interrupt him. Our primary responsibility when someone is speaking is to listen. When we feel the urge to interject, do the opposite and out-silence him. The argument is then over: the speaker doesn't have to raise the decibel level or keep repeating himself. He feels heard. We then get the chance to speak our Truth—to an attentive audience.

Above all, a person speaks to be heard. When we listen—and I mean truly listen, with full attention and without interruption—we are honoring that person and his Truth.

What Is Not Listening

Sometimes a person is not able to listen, or she has no real desire to listen. Yet she wants to create the illusion that she is listening. This is usually either out of fear or for manipulative purposes. Here are some other situations where one is not truly listening:

- Just being quiet.
- Appearing to be attentive.
- Suppressing feelings.
- Holding a response.
- Begrudgingly allowing another to speak.

Listening is being in calm, receptive, nonjudgmental silence, with no other motive than to create and maintain a space for another person to speak his Heartvoice.

To realize what a gift fully-present listening can be for someone, imagine that you are trying to express something and you can see that your audience isn't really listening. She keeps interrupting you and interjecting her own thoughts.

Now imagine a listener who is calm, focused on you, and nodding in recognition to what you are saying.

I don't think there is any question that you would feel disregarded in the first situation. You would undoubtedly sense that your Truth was being marginalized. With the second listener, you would feel that you were being held in regard, and that your Truth was being heard, no matter what the person's response to it.

BREAKING SILENCE

Responding with statements like "I disagree" or "What's the big deal?" is not Truthlistening. These are judgments and invitations for a reaction. When we are truly listening to someone and open to her Truth, we respond by acknowledging her Truth. This validates and empowers her. It is not our role to validate someone else's Truth by agreeing or disagreeing with it. We cannot make someone else's Truth right or wrong. The only time we need to resist someone else's Truthspeaking is if she is trying to push her Truth upon you.

Listening Exercises

The most effective methods I know of for honing silent listening skills are the *Shadowing exercises.* They reawaken the innate skills that our hunter-gatherer ancestors relied upon to move silently and inconspicuously while hunting and traversing dangerous territory. When we Shadow:

- We leave our own identity, thoughts and feelings behind.
- We become so absorbed and at-one with what we are shadowing that we move as he moves, think as he thinks, and feel as he feels.
- In doing so, we become as present, responsive—and unnoticeable—as a shadow.

In this state, we can best listen to whom we are shadowing, and best listen in general. We are fully attuned and have completely released ourselves of ego investiture. At the same time, our shadowing creates the ideal environment for others to express their Truths. They have an attentive, receptive audience that they can trust not to interrupt or judge.

The three exercises: *Shadow Walking, Shadow Miming and Shadow Talking,* work together synergistically to reawaken our innate shadowing ability. Along with this, they support our ability to remain connected and attuned with another person, which is one of the cornerstones of Truthlistening. Below I describe each exercise and offer suggestions for practicing them.

ASK PERMISSION

Shadowing is an interactive experience, so it may infringe on the personal space of others. When they are going to be consciously aware of your shadowing them, it is best to ask permission before beginning.

Shadow Walking

Here we slip into someone's wake and move synchronously with him, to the point where we become his shadow. To do it well, we place our attention wholly and inconspicuously on both the person and what draws his attention.

Unlike choreographed dance, where we are trained to move together, the Shadow Walker attunes herself to the person she is shadowing. She picks up subtle cues from both the person and the environment, telling her why, how and where he is going to move. She does not initiate movement; she responds to it.

Shadow walking can be easily practiced either indoors or out. Here are some tips:

- Randomly (and discreetly) fall in behind a person when he is walking or running by.

- The faster he is moving, the more distance you need to maintain between him and you.

- Watch for cues, such as where he is looking, how he shifts his weight, the length of his stride, how he places his steps, and any preoccupation he is involved in.

Shadow Miming

Imagine eating in front of a mirror and observing your image. It is Shadow Miming you, and this is exactly how to practice the exercise. In this expansion of Shadow Walking, we strengthen our listening skills by attuning even more to the subtle movements and gestures of a person's body language. We can Shadow Mime any behavior we observe in another person, which typically gives us more opportunities to practice it then Shadow Walking.

For some, meals turn out to be the most opportune time to practice Shadow Miming. Here is how to do it:

- Sit across from someone.

- Be her mirror, arranging your setting just like hers, adopting her posture, and mimicking her every movement.

- When you become proficient at the exercise, add the extra challenge of chewing as she does.

Warning: this exercise holds high entertainment value, so be prepared for some attention.

Shadow Talking

This is the most challenging of the three exercises, as it involves simultaneously saying what another person is speaking. The goal is not to have a delay between the other person's voice and ours, as with an echo, but rather to speak in sync with the voice. To effectively Shadow Talk, we need to expand our attention to include changes in vocal pitch, tone, and volume. Changing posture and facial expressions give further cues as to what the speaker might say next.-

Here are some pointers:

- The more quietly we speak, the easier Shadow Talking becomes. We have committed less vocal energy to what you are about to say, so we can more easily change course.

- It not only becomes more difficult to Shadow Talk the louder we speak, but the more disruptive and irritating it can become for the person we are shadowing.

- Silent Shadow Talking—which is much less irritating—can be practiced by either lip-synching or doing it entirely inwardly. Yet Shadow Talking is best learned by engaging your voice, so practice silently only after you have become proficient at doing it aloud.

- If we struggle too much when first attempting Shadow Talking, we can begin with Shadow Singing. Join in with someone singing a slow song you don't know. The melody, poetic structure, and repeated lyrics make singing easier to shadow than talking.

- We all continually repeat certain phrasings and structures of speech, so the more we Shadow Talk a certain individual, the easier it becomes. This helps give our undivided attention to the speaker.

GETTING BEYOND THE SELF

These Shadowing exercises help us remember that true listening happens only when we forget ourselves. Our filters, beliefs, prejudices, and preferences impede listening. Think of the perfect listener as a highly sensitive microphone that catches every nuance and background noise, then feeds it into a data storage unit, which can be accessed at any time to play back exactly what was input.

Practice these exercises at every opportunity. As with any new routines, the more we practice them, the more intuitive they become. And the more spontaneously present we will be with others.

Summary of Core Listening Practices

Before we go on to the next phase of Truthlistening, let's review what we have covered thus far. For ease of use, I'll present them in the form of tips:

- **Start listening fresh each moment**. When we bring the past into our presence, we keep hearing the same thing, no matter what is being said.

- **Find a distraction-free space and listen in silence.** A voice can be fully heard only in silence. Along with lack of noise, cultivate inner calm and receptiveness. Turn off your cellphone, take off your watch, turn your back to the clock on the wall.

- **Listen *deeply* to what is being said beyond words:** with tone of voice, posture, gesture, facial expression. Listen especially with your intuitive ears (see next chapter).

- **Listen with acceptance.** Judgment—the ego's reaction to another's Truth—distorts that Truth by injecting our perspective into it. Acceptance does not mean agreement, but rather openness to another view.

- **If it isn't working, take a Break.** Breathe, get up and stretch, and decide on a time to reconnect.

Support for Speakers

How can we as listeners best support clear and effective Truth-speaking? Whenever the speaker loses focus or we grow confused, we can break our silence and briefly facilitate. We need to be careful not to use this as an opening to react or analyze, but only to support the speaker's process. Here are some tips for doing so:

- **When needed, encourage the speaker to slow down** or pause periodically, to give space for comprehension and reflection.

- **If the speaker starts to drag on or meander off topic,** steer her back with a gentle reminder to cover only one topic at a time.

- **When there is unclarity, ask rather than second-guess.** Assumptions more often reflect our Truth than the speaker's.

- **Note the speaker's judgments and assumptions,** in case she would like to have them mirrored back.

- **Any input from us should relate only the speaker's Truth of the Now.**

Practicing these tips has the additional benefit of supporting the speaker by showing him that we are listening. Give guidance sparingly—and only when necessary—to minimize the risk of distracting or influencing the speaker.

Listening-with-Presence Exercise

Our core listening skills are innate, so in order to take full advantage of them, we need to know when they are functioning optimally. I have designed the following exercise to help you do this. One or more people can participate, and you will need a storyteller and a timekeeper. Here are the steps:

1. **Have someone tell you a story** that is meaningful to him and lasts about twelve minutes.

2. **Listen to the first three minutes while working on a project,** such as a craft, sewing, or preparing a meal.
3. **Listen for the next three minutes with your back to the storyteller.**
4. **Face the storyteller for the next three minutes,** sitting more than a body-length away.
5. **Sit directly in front of the storyteller for the last three minutes,** making eye contact, leaning forward, nodding, and saying *"hmm" periodically to acknowledge your listening.*
6. **Relate the story back to the storyteller** and see which segment(s) you remember best.

You will probably find, as did M. Scott Peck (author of *The Road Less Traveled*), that "You cannot truly listen to anyone and do anything else at the same time."[10]

The Chapter at a Glance

There is no Truthspeaking without Truthlistening. We can speak our Truths until we are blue in the face, yet if nobody listens—or knows *how* to listen—we might as well save our breaths. In effect, nothing was spoken. A voice needs an open and accepting ear to receive it. Traditional Hawaiians express it this way: He lohe ke ola, he kuli ka make—*To hear is life, to turn a deaf ear is death.*[11]

If we cannot hear our Truths, we cannot voice them. And if we cannot hear the Truths of others, we cannot honor them. The term *Truthspeaking* could fairly be called a misnomer, as listening is the fundamental process. We are mostly silent, yet we listen all of the time. In our culture, much is said of taking personal responsibility for what we say; however, not for how we listen. We think of listening as a simple mechanical process, where it is a skill of the highest order.

Listening is being in calm, receptive, nonjudgmental silence with no other motive than to create and maintain space for another person to speak her Heartvoice. Listening is a more effective way of being heard than speaking itself. When we listen respectfully and attentively, we create an environment for being heard. Listeners give us perspective and reflections of ourselves. When we listen to each other, everybody is heard—including us.

We listen best in silence. Although we tend to believe that silence is merely the absence of speech, engaged silence creates a sense of presence that says more than any words could. The act of sitting with someone in silence fosters trust and rapport. It is a tangible sign of interest and commitment.

We honor another's truth by listening to it in conscious silence, rather than biting our tongues and waiting for our first opportunity to speak. Silence gives us the space to be as a question: receptive to what we see, feel, sense, and intuit. We offer an invitation for another to speak from her Heart, and we honor her voice by listening without debate, reaction, or judgment.

Part of what we hear is the silences before, between and after the words. Anticipation, feeling, and reaction are conveyed in the silences rather than the words. The setting, facial expressions, body language, relationship to the speaker, history with the subject matter, and so much more, are spoken by silence. As well, the speaker reads our sincerity, sense of presence, and reactions in our silence.

As we listen, it is not for us to agree or disagree with someone else's Truth. Everybody has their own Truths, and whether or not they resonate with ours does not make them right or wrong. The only time Truthspeakers need to resist others' Truths is when they are trying to force their Truths upon someone else.

Chapter Six Endnotes

1   Mary Kawena Pukui, *'Ōlelo No'eau, Hawaiian Proverbs and Poetical Sayings,* 84.

2   John Lahr, *Up Against the Fourth Wall: Essays on Modern Theater,* (Random House, 1970), 75.

3   Charles Alexander Eastman, *The Soul of an Indian and Other Writings from Ohiyesa*, ed. Kent Nerburn (New World Library, 1993), 89.

4   *Native American Wisdom*, ed. Kent Nerburn and Louise Mengel-koch (New World Library, 1991), 8-9.

5   Haunani-Kay Trask, *From a Native Daughter: Colonialism and Sovereignty in Hawaii*, (University of Hawaii Press, 1999), 118.

6   I. Opie and P. Opie, *The Oxford Dictionary of Nursery Rhymes* (Oxford: Oxford University Press, 1951), 403.

7   Charles Alexander Eastman, *Indian Scout Craft and Lore* (New York: Dover Publications, 1914), 152.

8   Stanislaw J. Lec, *Unkempt Thoughts*, (St. Martin's Press, 1965), 55.

9   Roger E. Axtell, *Gestures: The Do's and Taboos of Body Language Around the World* (Wiley, 2008), 2.

10 Scott Peck, *The Road Less Traveled* (Arrow Books, 1978), 125.

11 Mary Kawena Pukui, *'Ōlelo No'eau, Hawaiian Proverbs and Poetical Sayings,* 84.

CHAPTER SEVEN

INTUITIVE LISTENING: TAPPING INTO THE UNIVERSAL LANGUAGE

Maani Assinewe, a Canadian Ojibwe who is one of my Elders, told me the story about her mother, who was one day sitting alone and sewing. She tried and tried to thread a needle, but just couldn't do it.

"Eh, it seems like you're having trouble there with that needle," came a voice from the other side of the room. Maani's mother jumped with a start and said, "How long have you been here?"

"For a while," the visitor replied. "I guess you didn't hear me come in. Hand me that," she said, and she ran the thread through the eye of the needle with no problem.

The visitor was blind, yet she knew what Maani's mother was doing and what was needed. Now that is listening! The blind woman had evolved her senses to the point that they worked together synchronously to help her see—sometimes better than a person with sight. This is the way with intuitive listening, which involves not just hearing, but all of the senses, along with what can be heard beyond sound.

In the previous chapter, we learned how listening in calm, receptive, nonjudgmental silence helps create space for Truth to emerge. This is the space needed for intuition to help us fully hear Truth.

Defining Intuition

The Latin term *intueri*, is generally translated as *to contemplate* or *to gaze upon.* Turned inward, this gaze spontaneously resurfaces as our intuitive voice. This is our natural ability to grasp insight and meaning quickly, without need for reason or analysis. Intuition goes by many names: *mental telepathy, psychic ability, extrasensory perception, gut feeling, first impression, nonverbal communication, the primal language,* and *interspecies communication.* In my book *Becoming Nature* (Bear & Company, 2016), I call it *Naturespeak,* which is the word I learned from my Elders. Each term describes an aspect of intuition.

In the context of Truthlistening, intuition takes the form of what I call *Heart-to-Heart* listening. This is the First Language— the mother tongue of all life and the foundation of communication within and between species. We listen intuitively to and from the Heart because it is the seat of our Truth, and because it emanates beyond our bodies. The human heart has a powerful electromagnetic field of its own that is several times stronger than the brain's, and which can be detected by scientific equipment from several feet away.[1]

German philosopher Frederick Nietzsche coined the phrase *third ear* to describe our intuitive ability to hear the metaphorical language of dreams and the Heartvoice.[2] With our third ear, we can hear between and beyond words, so that we can grasp what somebody intends to say, whether or not he is able to completely verbalize it.

THE INTUITIVE VOICE OF DREAMS

The voice of our superconscious self (also known as greater self, guardian angel, spirit guide, or animal guide) is often heard in dreams. The Heartvoice that we express when Truthspeaking holds much in common with our Dreamvoice. Both come from our center, have strong intuitive components, are non-calculating and sincere, and can be trusted by both ourselves and others. They complement each other, with the Heartvoice giving immediate guidance by day and the Dreamvoice giving reflective guidance by night. The fundamental difference between the two is that only the Heartvoice includes our ego, as it goes dormant while we sleep.

Whispers Beyond Words

If we were to consciously dwell on every letter, word, sentence, and grammatical structure involved in speaking or writing, our communication would be severely hampered.[3] Our ability to communicate fluently is due to the fact that intuition is the foundation of verbal communication. Spoken and written language alone are limited because they can only approximate the intuitive component.

Behind every word is a learned association that gives it meaning. The word is merely a symbol, with communication occurring only if the symbols connect with an impulse, memory, or feeling. This takes us into the realm of nonverbal communication, which if you'll remember from the previous chapter, comprises the bulk of discourse.

Whether or not we consciously recognize nonverbal cues, we continually intuit and interpret them. We gauge others' emotional states before they ever speak a word. We decide how to best broach topics by impressions we receive from facial expression, demeanor, posture, movement, and dress. Sometimes our cues come from extrasensory perception, such as when we have a hunch about something or feel that we are being watched.

Intuition speaks subtly, yet it speaks much more quickly than the rational mind, and it can be trusted. In one study, participants played a game with two stacks of cards, one of which was rigged against them. Fifty cards into the game, players started to become consciously aware of this fact—however, just *ten* cards into the game, the sweat glands on their palms opened whenever they reached for the rigged deck.[4]

We react similarly on an intuitive level when randomly exposed to either neutral or emotionally charged images on a computer screen—seconds *before* the computer has selected the image.[5] A similar effect is found in experiments using sound instead of visual images.[6] Perhaps this points to the basis of our premonitional ability.

Much like the heart's electromagnetic field, our intuitive abilities show us that we already exist in deep connection with others. We communicate in ways that the rational mind cannot perceive or fully explain. When we acknowledge our capacity to listen intuitively and give it space, we are able to live in greater attunement with the Web of Life.

Unfortunately, modern life has led us to lose touch with our intuitive abilities. In defining ourselves as a rational species, we have created a world where nearly everything has to be quantifiable and defined with words. Intuition, which cannot be fully quantified and transcends words, is unintelligible in the language of this culture. We treat intuition as unknowable, when in fact it was the *first* thing our species knew. Despite the power that intuition can grant us, it currently reaches many of us only in muffled whispers.

When we embraced the identity of rationality, we allowed our perceptive and intuitive abilities to atrophy. We can see the process reenacted in our children. A fundamental part of early childhood development is the domestication process, which consists of connecting children with reality—that is, reality according to the rational mind. Through positive and negative reinforcement, children internalize our interactive ethos: speak or be spoken to. They eventually quit listening to the family dog and the birds outside, and they forget the time when they could intuit Truth without needing words.

However, what lies dormant can reawaken—we do not lose what is innate.

AN EXERCISE TO STRENGTHEN INTUITION

Play a team sport or game that requires coordinated effort, quick thinking, and fast decision-making. For effectiveness, it's important to play at least once a week. Over time, you should notice yourself more and more easily sliding into now-consciousness as soon as you start the game. The more weeks you play, the easier it becomes to switch back and forth from reflective to intuitive thinking.

Our Two Minds

We typically refer to the working mind as a singular entity. Yet we can distinguish between two distinct components: the *limbic system* and the *neocortex*. The seat of our subconscious is the limbic system, which is also known as the *old* or *intuitive mind*. It governs social processing, behavior, long-term memory, pain and pleasure, motivation, and our fight-flight mechanism. It is the source of our gut feelings, attractions and repulsions, and all of those urges that are hard to explain or resist.

The neocortex is commonly called the *new brain* or *rational mind*. In simplified terms, it is the seat of deliberate, analytical thought, and it governs language and our spatial sense. The rational mind, which is found in a high state of development only in mammals, evolved as an adjunct to the intuitive mind, to give it additional range and scope for the complexities of group survival and the hunt. The rational mind gives us our shoulds and shouldn'ts, our planning and projecting—the studied approach to life.

When we receive sensory input, it gets directed either to the intuitive mind or the rational mind. With verbal input—our primary contemporary source of information—going to the rational mind, we have come to view it as the doorway to truth and understanding. This is made possible in part by the fact that we Humans have what may be the highest rational-to-intuitive-mind ratio of all mammals. Having come to see ourselves as essentially rational, verbally oriented beings, we have directed our rational minds to largely take over our lives.

It is not the rational mind itself, but our overdependence on it, that restricts our ability to listen intuitively. This gives us a serious handicap, as the rational mind can process barely one-twentieth of the input that the intuitive mind is capable of. Only 1-5% of our decisions and actions are conscious; the rest originate intuitively.[7] The intuitive mind remains critical to our daily functioning, even if we are not fully aware of it.

TO REVITALIZE THE INTUITIVE MIND

1 **Embark** *on an experience (a walk, daytrip, shopping...) without a goal in mind.*
2 **Accept** *all turns in the road.*
3 **Go** *where you feel guided.*
4 **Cherish** *whatever the experience brings.*

Instead of saying turn left or it's on my right while traveling, use north, south, east, and west. It automatically switches our analytical mindset to intuitive.

Intuition and the Web of Life

When we allow the rational mind to serve the intuitive mind—in other words, when we let the mind serve the Heart—we can easily discern our Truth and the Truths of others. A force more powerful than analytical thinking guides us toward the Heartvoice.

With the intuitive mind, we break out of our culture's antagonistic dichotomy of *either speak or be spoken to*. A deep connection—Heart-to-Heart—can then occur. Recent research has found that when we are forced to make quick decisions, based on intuition alone, we are more cooperative and less self-focused than when decisions are made after extended reflection.[8]

Intuitive listening makes it impossible to *just* talk to others or to *just* listen to what they say. *Intuitive communication is spontaneous, with listening and speaking occurring simultaneously and indistinguishably from each other.* The listener and speaker together become synchronously functioning organs in a great organism, the *Web of Life*. We each become fully present and responsive to the energies at play, where before I was an observer with my own agenda. Like a Rabbit who relaxes when Fox tells him she isn't hungry, we harmoniously meld with the Web.

As our intuitive listening skills develop, we find ourselves becoming attuned to non-human members of the Web of Life, as they already live and speak their Truth in the Now. Listening is listening, whether it be to a human, an animal, or the wind. With all of them, we can employ the same listening skills to great advantage.

One of the beauties of Truthlistening is that we are tuning in to the speaker without expectation, and on her own terms. This gives us the opportunity to sensitize to the range of communication that occurs beyond the verbal, human-style communication to which we are accustomed.

AN EXERCISE FOR TUNING IN

It takes time and practice in order to fully intuit what the other animals communicate. A helpful first step we can take is to realize that whatever we think and feel affects the creatures around us. Accepting personal responsibility for this psycho-emotional influence of ours is the cornerstone to having functional relationships—especially in Nature. As well, this is an acknowledgement of our conscious participation in the Web of Life.

You've probably heard about people who can talk with animals (commonly known as animal communicators), and perhaps you know one. In actuality, they connect in the intuition-based language beyond words that Truthlistening opens to us. This language is centered around relationship. Research indicates that intuitive communication occurs between humans and other animals, and that it is enhanced with affection.[9] In the following chapter, we learn more about this by exploring empathy—the force that sustains relationships built on Truthlistening.

The Chapter at a Glance

In the previous chapter we learned how listening in calm, receptive, nonjudgmental silence helps create space for Truth to emerge. For Truth to be fully heard, we must then listen intuitively.

Mental telepathy, psychic ability, extrasensory perception (ESP), gut feeling, first impressions, nonverbal communication, animal talk, the primal language, and interspecies communication are all terms for intuition. Each one describes an aspect of intuition, yet not one of these fully captures what it is.

I like the term _Heart-to-Heart listening_, which directly states what it is, rather than trying to explain it. _Heart-to-Heart listening_ is the First Language—the mother tongue of all life and the foundation of interspecies communication. German philosopher Frederick Nietzsche, coined the phrase _third ear_ to describe the intuitive Heartvoice.[10]

Intuition is already part of our communication. Fluent verbal interaction depends on our ability to automatically intuit linguistic meaning and structure. We regularly intuit nonverbal cues, which comprise the bulk of communication.

Unfortunately, modern life has caused us to lose touch with a good share of our intuitive abilities. By defining ourselves as a rational species, we have created a world where nearly everything has to be quantifiable and defined with words. Intuition, which transcends words and cannot be fully quantified, becomes unintelligible to us. We treat it as unknowable, when in fact it was our species' primal form of communication. Fortunately, we still have this ability, as we cannot lose what is innate.

We often refer to the human brain as a singular organ, yet we can distinguish between two distinct parts: the _limbic system:_ the seat of intuition, and the _neocortex:_ which gives us our analytical abilities. The neocortex, which is only found in mammals, evolved as an adjunct to the intuitive mind, to give it additional range for the complexities of survival and the hunt.

We humans, who have what may be the highest rational-to-intuitive-mind ratio of all mammals, have come to see ourselves as _only_ rational, verbally oriented beings. This has caused us to neglect our deeper intuitive abilities. However, when we allow the rational mind to serve the intuitive mind— i.e., when we let the mind to serve the Heart—we can more easily discern our Heartvoice and the Heartvoice of others.

As our intuitive listening skills awaken, we will discover that we are naturally attuned to the other members of the Web of Life, as they already live and speak their Truth in the Now. Listening is listening, whether it be to a human, another animal, or the wind. With all of them, we can employ the same beyond-words listening skills that Truthlistening brings us. It's all about relationship.

Next we look at the force that sustains Truthlistening-based relationships: empathy.

Chapter Seven Endnotes

1   R. McCraty, M. Atkinson, and R.T. Bradley, "Electrophysiological Evidence of Intuition, Part 1: The Surprising Role of the Heart," *Journal of Alternative and Complementary Medicine* 10, no. 1 (2004): 133-43.

2   Friedrich Nietzsche, *Beyond Good and Evil* (New York: Carlton House, 1960), 180-1.

3   Eugene Sadler-Smith, *Inside Intuition* (Routledge, 2012), 7.

4   Antoine Bechara et al., "Deciding Advantageously Before Knowing the Advantageous Strategy," *Science* 275, no. 5304 (1997): 1293-5.

5   D.I. Radin, "Unconscious Perception of Future Emotions: An Experiment in Presentiment," *Journal of Scientific Exploration* 11 (1997): 163-80.

6   S. James Spottiswoode and E. C. May, "Skin Conductance Prestimulus Response: Analyses, Artifacts and a Pilot Study." *Journal of Scientific Exploration* 17, no. 4 (2003): 617-41.

7   Daniel Goleman et al, *Measuring the Immeasurable: the Scientific Case for Spirituality* (Boulder, Sounds True, 2008), 192.

8   David G. Rand, Joshua D. Greene, and Martin A. Nowak, "Spontaneous Giving and Calculated Greed." *Nature* 489, no. 7416 (2012): 427-430.

CHAPTER EIGHT

LISTENING WITH PERSPECTIVE

Truthlistening is empathy, which is the foundation of any meaningful relationship or connection with another person. The more empathetic I am, the closer I feel to somebody, and the less likely I am to judge or be reactive. When I listen with empathy, I relate to the speaker in the Now and from the Heart. Long ago, an anonymous Shoshone nicely described what it's like: "Oh, the comfort, the inexpressible comfort of feeling safe with a person, having neither to weigh thought nor measure words, but pouring them all right out, just as they are, chaff and grain together, certain that a faithful hand will take and sift them, keep what is worth keeping, and with a breath of kindness, blow the rest away."[1]

We often place too much emphasis on *active listening* over Truthlistening. Marital researcher Dr. John Gottman has found that active listening in conflict resolution does not in and of itself lead to a successful relationship.[2] More important, he found, is removing the specific feelings of contempt, belligerence, and defensiveness from that listening.[3] I call this *separating fact from feeling*.

Listening from a caring, open place matters more so than the style of our communication We might be able to listen while being deeply agitated; however, it is not Truthlistening. Empathy is what transforms active listening into Truthlistening, and empathy cannot penetrate the wall of heavy emotion. This chapter helps us bridge the chasm between our willingness to listen to being able to listen empathetically. Here is the four-step transition:

1. **Discern the context** of the conversation, not the facts.

2. **Clarify the core emotions** (see Chapter 10) behind any reactive feelings.

3. **Remain detached from the outcome** of the conversation.

4. **Establish an empathetic connection** with the speaker.

1: Discerning Context

To begin with, it is most important to know what the speaker intends to talk about. While this may seem obvious and straightforward, it requires attention, in order to avoid empathizing with a False Truth.

Identifying context requires separating observations from their presentation as *facts*. In Chapter 3 we discussed how observations become False Truth when they are presumed to be facts and remain unquestioned. However, *when speakers acknowledge observations as tentative and personal, they provide important contextual information for listeners.*

REMEMBERING THE CIRCLE WAY

When we address context or circumstances rather than facts, we move closer to the Circle Way. The word circumstance *comes from the Latin* circumstāre, *meaning to gather around in a circle. Just as Truth is personal and ever-changing, it takes many individuals, each with a different perspective, to form a circle that is whole.*

Let's return to the damaged Tomahawk example in Chapter 4. You'll remember that someone in one of our primitive camps loaned out a tomahawk that was later returned damaged. As it turns out, the Tomahawk was damaged by a third person who used it without permission. If the owner assumed that the original borrower damaged her Tomahawk, she would have been declaring an observation as fact—a False Truth—rather than describing the context or circumstance.

juxhtaydf kzzdfd eE

Speaking contextually, she could have said, "I loaned out my tomahawk, and now I see that it is damaged." She would have shared the circumstances motivating her to speak which would have given the listener the information necessary to connect with the speaker's actual Truth.

2: Clarifying Core Emotions

Now we need to know where to direct our empathy. We do this by separating the speaker's reactive feeling from the core emotion it masks. The terms *feeling* and *emotion* are often used interchangeably, while I consider a feeling to be the surface manifestation of an underlying emotional state.

While how we feel can vary in response to a glance, a hand on the shoulder, or being hungry, a core emotion (such as longing) is less volatile. Surface feelings should be acknowledged, and at the same time let's remember that they come and go like clouds over the sun. Empathizing with them may provide temporary relief for the speaker, yet it is holding space for core emotions that help guide the speaker's Truth to be communicated.

Overemphasis on the speaker's reactive feelings distorts our perceptions and creates imaginings, or what is known in the mental health field as *cognitive* or *memory distortions* (more on this in my book *Breaking the Trauma Code*). In order to get back to pure perception, we need to abandon our distortions. If we don't, we create False Truths.

To Distinguish Reactive Feelings from Core Emotions

When you are the speaker, use this modified version of the Chapter 4 technique for avoiding manipulative speech:

1. **Acknowledge your feeling** about an issue.
2. **Recognize the imagining** you have embraced because of this feeling.
3. **Determine what lies behind the imagining** by asking, "What am I trying to get?"

4. **Follow your need down to the core emotion** from which it arose (see Chapter 10).

5. **Express your core emotion.** This is your Truth.

6. **Have someone succinctly reflect your Truth back to you,** in order to clarify it.

When you are the listener and sense that reactive feelings are masking the speaker's Truth:

1. **Express your awareness** and ask the speaker if you may help clarify his Truth.

2. **Ask him to identify what he is feeling.**

3. **Ask what need underlies the feeling.** Be careful to respect the feeling. If needed, help him connect with the need.

4. **Ask what core emotion is creating the need.**

5. **Suggest that he embrace the core emotion** rather than the reactive feeling.

6. **Return to respectful silence.**

Some listeners think they help the speaker express his Truth by addressing just the reactive feeling or dysfunctional communication pattern. They often address the speaker with lines like, "What is your fear?" or "I think you're sounding victimized." By putting the focus on the reactive feelings, this approach diminishes or negates the speaker's Truth.

I don't know of a more sure way to diminish perspective than allowing reactive feelings to dominate a conversation (see Chapter 12). And I don't know of a better way to stay centered in our Heart-of-Hearts and listen with clear empathy than to separate reactive feelings from the speaker's or listener's Truth.

In addition to the above techniques, give this one a try. When you have options, you can choose the one that best fits the situation. This is the one my working partners and I use most.

1. **Separate** fact from feeling, i.e. distinguish the feeling or reactive pattern from the Truth.

2. **Recognize** and respond to feeling.
3. **Wait** until the emotional charge has dissipated before addressing the Truth.

3: Detaching from Outcome

When listening, we sometimes feel drawn to speculate, project, plan, worry, or fantasize. At other times, we listen with vested interests or desired outcomes. Any of this distances us from the speaker by dishonoring his Truth. In effect, we distort it by running it through the filters of our personal needs and wants.

In addition, we can distort the speaker's Truth when we are triggered by something he says. Attached to a trigger is usually a reactive pattern, which distorts what is said to fit the pattern. If we are in victim mode, we're going to find a way to feel victimized by whatever is said. If we are externalizing, we're going to twist what is said to cause someone else to feel responsible and guilty.

When we engage in patterned listening instead of empathetic listening, it's as though we go on automatic pilot and field whatever comes at us with our pre-programming. I call this *reflex listening*. When we are in this state, we are not fully present, which means we cannot truly listen.

This disconnect occurs when we listen from the rational mind, rather than intuitively. We withdraw from the present moment and attach to a future outcome—even with the high cost of the Now, the birthplace of Truth.

Here I am reminded of the words of ninth-century Zen master Huang-po, who said, "Many people are afraid to empty their own minds lest they plunge into the Void. Ha! What they don't realize is that their own mind *is* the Void."[4] What we cling to so tenaciously and call knowledge actually shows our ignorance. What we claim to be intelligence only exposes our arrogance and disconnectedness.

When we listen with the intuitive mind and enter into conversation with a questioning mindset, we create space within ourselves for what the person is going to express. To receive the speaker's Truth with clarity and empathy, both speaker and listener must be in the same moment—*this* moment.

4: Establishing Empathy

At this point, it becomes important to understand how empathy is distinct from both sympathy and compassion.

Sympathy can be offered or withheld. As such, it places the listener in a position of power over the speaker. Compassion, on the other hand, has the listener relinquishing his power, as he becomes subsumed in the speaker's emotional state. Empathy is not something we offer; it is something we *do*. Unlike sympathy and compassion, which take on feelings, empathy works like a light that shines *through* feelings to illuminate the Truth behind them.

Sympathy and compassion each correspond to a manner of listening that is distinct from empathetic listening, as here outlined:

Qualities of Listening

Type of Listening	Qualities	Example
Sympathetic	Identifying with the feelings of the other person.	I am sorry for how disconnected you are feeling.
Compassionate	Identifying with *and* experiencing the feelings of the other person.	I am feeling your disconnection and how overwhelming it is.
Empathetic	Recognizing the feelings of the other person and discerning the Truth behind them.	I can sense how disconnected you feel. Are you impatient with your progress compared to the rest of the group?

When we listen sympathetically, we do two things that mask the speaker's Truth: we attach emotionally to the speaker, and we assume a superior position. Some people are convinced that compassion is the noble way to listen, yet it is nothing more than deep sympathy.

Both approaches often lead to rescuing, and sometimes worse: a codependent relationship. Here speaker and listener become entangled to the point where they each lose their sense of self and have trouble functioning independently.

VIRTUOUS ACTIONS?

Sympathetic and compassionate listening provides an avenue for manipulating others to achieve a desired outcome through actions that seem virtuous. This occurs both consciously and inadvertently. Here are examples, along with healthy alternatives:

Virtuous Action	Hidden Attachment Motivation	Non-attachment Alternative
Sympathy	Superiority. When I sympathize, I assume that I am more privileged.	Empathy
Forgiveness	Judgment. When I forgive, I come from a place of moral superiority.	Acceptance
Gift-giving	Control—if I have concern for how it is used or who ultimately possesses it.	Gifting with no strings attached
Advice	Conversion—if I am influencing someone to think or do as I would.	Listening, mirroring

On the other hand, *empathetic listening allows us to be emotionally sensitive without getting attached.* We can remain dissociated from any outcome and centered in our Heart-of-Hearts. This keeps us separated from the speaker's Truth, which helps us to easily honor it.

"I don't understand how you can remain unattached without becoming insensitive," a Truthspeaking workshop participant once commented. I replied that empathy in action is showing someone how to fish rather than continually giving her fish. It is seeing the wisdom in allowing a child to learn by his mistakes, rather than protecting him by rescuing and enabling him. It is caring without controlling, feeling without taking on feelings, and listening without judging or interjecting.

"That sounds good," was the reply, "but how is it actually done?" By pulling our Truth out from under the emotional overlay that often disguises it. As Truthlisteners, our job is to keep from vicariously experiencing another's feelings. We create a space to honor the expression of those feelings, while discerning the Truth that lies behind them. *When we show genuine interest by being fully present and encouraging, without forming opinions or becoming emotionally engulfed, we are listening empathetically.*

Now that we have covered the fundamentals for listening from the Heart, we can go on to the next chapter and learn how to summon the one element that makes it all possible: the courage to truly listen.

The Chapter at a Glance

Truthlistening is empathy. It is the foundation of any meaningful exchange with another person, and it is vital to a healthy relationship. The more empathetic we are, the closer we feel to somebody, and the less likely we are to judge or be reactively triggered. When we listen with empathy, we connect with the speaker in the Now and from the Heart.

Many of us place emphasis on active listening. Empathy transforms it into Truthlistening. We can still be listening actively when we are critical or manipulative; however, this is not Truthlistening.

The first step in empathetic listening is to determine the circumstances of the conversation. This involves separating observations from their gloss as *facts.* In Chapter 4, we discussed how observations can lead us toward False Truths when they are presumed to be facts and remain unquestioned. When we identify and acknowledge observations as tentative and personal, the listener is given the necessary contextual information.

Next, we need to separate the speaker's reactive feelings from the core emotions that they mask. We often hear *feelings* and *emotions* used interchangeably, yet for our process here, we need to distinguish one from the other. Feelings are the ever-changing surface ripples caused by the expression of our core emotions: fear and longing. While feelings can change over something as slight as a glance, a touch on the shoulder, or the sight of a sweet roll, emotions are stable and long-held. Empathizing with feelings may give the speaker temporary comfort, yet it is empathizing with his core emotions that helps guide him to his Truth.

While listening, we may feel drawn to speculate, project, plan, worry, or fantasize. With any of these, we listen through a vested-interest filter, which dishonors the speaker's Truth by distorting it. To listen empathetically, we must detach from the outcome and remain centered in the Now.

Let's be careful about confusing empathy with sympathy or compassion. Sympathy can be offered and withheld, which gives the listener power over the speaker. Compassion, on the other hand, has the listener relinquishing his power, to become subsumed in the speaker's emotional state.

Empathy is not something we offer; it is something we do. Unlike sympathy and compassion, which engage with feelings, empathy works *through* to the other side of them, where the speaker's Truth resides.

Chapter Eight Endnotes

1   *Native American Wisdom*, ed. Kent Nerburn and Louise Mengelkoch (New World Library, 1991), 37.

2   John Mordechai Gottman and Nan Silver, *The Seven Principles for Making Marriage Work* (New York: Crown, 1999), 12.

3   John M. Gottman et al., "Predicting Marital Happiness and Stability from Newlywed Interactions." *Journal of Marriage and the Family* (1998): 17.

4   John Blofeld, *The Zen Teaching of Huang Po, On the Transmission of Mind* (New York: Grove Wedenfeld, 1958), 48.

CHAPTER NINE

AND ABOVE ALL, COURAGE

We take a risk by opening our Hearts and extending trust every time we Truthlisten. This takes courage. Keeping our Hearts open to Truth and detached from the outcome—this takes even more courage.

Yet, there is no other way, as an open Heart without the daring to keep it open is like a bird without wings. The Truthlistening journey asks that we embrace the bitter as well as the sweet of what Truth brings. To pick and choose would be to live a False Truth.

This requires trust with risk: adventuring from the security of knowing to the frontier of the unknown. It is having faith that we are capable of communicating in a better way. It is having the self-love to believe that we are worthy of being happy and content with life.

For many of us, it takes not only courage, but *tremendous* courage, to open the door and step out into these nebulous winds—into our personal frontier.

When we do, we strip away habit, pretense, and illusion. We occupy the place that encourages us to be fully present and aware, to be finely attuned and sensitized. Our personal frontier is where we find our Truth. It takes courage to get there, yet once we arrive, this vibrant, unfettered state of being renews our will to keep going.

Letting Go

The experience of Truthlistening is a continual explosion of the Now. At the same time, the more we immerse ourselves in the present Truth, the further we drift from whence we came. As uplifting as our new life is becoming, the pangs of our life left behind can be equally devastating.

Some of us will feel destabilized during the transition. We may end up romanticizing our past and its old comforts, and yearning for the people and places we knew, even though in the past they were nothing particularly desirable. They may have been the very things that kept us from our frontier.

At this point, some of us rationalize our way into abandoning the quest and finding contentment in things as they are. We create an illusion that makes forsaking the quest appear to be the quest itself. Only deep inside we keep being troubled by the nagging feeling that comes from knowing we are here in this life to realize our limits, then reach beyond them.

FINDING OUR LIMITS

We can begin to release our clutch on the past by asking ourselves:

1 *What or who repels me?*
2 *What or who holds power over me?*
3 *What or who causes me to forget who I am?*
4 *What or who continually triggers feelings of anger, jealousy, or abandonment?*

At first, it will likely feel uncomfortable to sit with the answers. What they offer us, though, is the invaluable chance to see our limits. Then we can invoke our courage to confront them.

What we perceive as our limit is in actuality only the threshold between the known and the unknown. A river is a limit only because we haven't yet figured out a way to cross it. And it will remain a limit if we don't have the courage to do so, or if we convince ourselves that we don't have the wherewithal to do it.

Courage in Relationship

Re-becoming a Truthlistener is a life-changing experience. Leaving the old, familiar chitchat and pretense behind and getting down to the Heart of communication is fundamentally a journey of self-discovery. What inevitably follows is a reformulation of relationship as we know it. Creating trust in a Truthlistening-based relationship starts with presence. Yes, the warmth of the past is soothing, yet it leaves us disconnected from the Now.

Along with letting go of the bygone, we must release the urge to seek *compatible relationships*. They can be safe and comfortable, yet they are typically not very stimulating or growth-oriented. This is because we have chosen mirror images of ourselves. These partners reinforce who we are (or at least the illusion we are comfortable with), without having much new to offer. They stay with us in familiar territory, and seldom is there mention of venturing out on our personal frontiers.

When we emerge from behind our boundaries, everything becomes new and anything is possible. There is where we meet other people on their frontiers, and there is where *complementary relationships* are born.

Think of compatible relationships as butter on butter and complementary relationships as butter on toast. Rather than being threatened by differences in background, perspective, or ways of doing things, we burn with a yearning to hear their stories and learn from them. We are stimulated and inspired by change and new direction.

WE JOURNEY ALONGSIDE OTHERS

Remember: we are social beings. We are not designed to sustain ourselves alone out on our frontiers, even though we need to venture there alone. Engaging there takes energy, and it can be fatiguing. At the same time, however, it is giving. Fortunately, what venturing forth costs us is more than compensated for by what we gain.

In our boundaried existence, we learned to shun change, as it caused weakness and pain. On the flipside, our ever-changing personal Truths make us ever-changing beings, which gives us our dynamic nature and allows us to be fully engaged with the ever-fluctuating Web of Life.

As we move in this new direction, we may be tempted to attach it to a particular philosophy or belief system. From a Truthlistening perspective, this is likely a fear-based response to being out on the frontier of the unknown. We have an anxiety-driven compulsion to explain the unexplainable, to make the infinite into the finite, and to tame an aimless ramble on the frontier with words.

Philosophies and beliefs appear to give a sense of purpose to the indefinable journey; yet if we found the courage and the tools to walk it, these principles would all of a sudden become as extraneous and cumbersome as a wetsuit to a duck.

HOLDING ONTO CURIOSITY

In my survival training workshops, I can tell those who are ready to meet their frontiers by merely describing a crisis situation that goes beyond their experience. They listen intently, then envision the situation and imagine how they might respond.

They exhibit the same approach in the field. Almost to a person, they turn out to be the ones who give it their all and pull through in tough situations. This is even though it is outside their realm of experience, and even though it takes them beyond what they considered their limits.

Most of them do not act out of a sense of guilt or responsibility, but rather they are intrigued by what might lie out on their frontiers, and they yearn to discover it. The same applies to Truthlistening, as it takes each of us to the same personal frontier—there is only one. So we need to Truthlisten with the same sense of wonder and longing for what might be possible as we would for any other frontier venture.

Where Courage Takes Us

To illustrate what it might be like to embrace our fear and venture into our personal frontier, here is a dialogue I had with a trainee in one of the guardian-warrior programs I teach:

Trainee: For me it's hard to figure out the point where it's getting dangerous. How do you distinguish the boundary between self-protectiveness and going out in your frontier? I'm concerned about stepping out too far and hurting myself.

Tamarack: That's a tough question, and the only way to get the answer is to go there. You may need to hurt yourself, by pushing and going what seems to be too far. *As long as it's not life-threatening or harmful to your overall physical or emotional health.* You get wet, you get cold, you get a little stressed; so what? It's your frontier—you need to go there. You'll then be able to recognize whether it is actually because you have pushed too far, or whether it's because you are not attuned and fear has gripped you, narrowing your perspective.

Trainee: Is my fear different from my sense of caution?

Tamarack: The two *are* different—and also related. When we are cautious, oftentimes it is based upon what worked and did not work for us in the past. When we take what we have gained from the past and use that to chart our future, all we are doing is reliving the past. *We are limiting what our future can be by what our past has been.* And, like living by fear alone, that keeps us from going out on our frontier. Caution both tames our frontier and leads us to it in a guarded way. All we are venturing out on, then, is an illusion. If it is not a place of the unknown, a place of risk and surprises, it is not a frontier.

Trainee: I'm not sure I know how to stop being so cautious all at once.

Tamarack: Remember that a journey is one step at a time. Take that first step and put everything you have into it. Don't worry about whether you have enough energy for the next step, or for later in the day. Just get immersed right in the here and now. The better you can take care of that one thing, the better you will be able to take care the next thing, and the next.

Trainee: I'm so used to not even considering that possibility, though.

Tamarack: I'd like to stress here the beauty of the fact that we are creatures of habit and pattern. We can either see ourselves as being controlled and victimized by our habits, or we can turn it around and establish functional habits to support our exploring. The real gift from our training here is that if we can gain awareness and proficiency in one arena, it spills into all arenas. If I can learn to take care of myself when I'm cold and wet, I can take care of myself in many other situations.

Trainee: Why am I so worried about this first step, then?

Tamarack: Perhaps because at the start of every journey is inertia. You have a vision, and taking that first step is the hardest because you're translating potential energy into kinetic. That initial step is what gets your mass moving, gets you over your inertia. Then the second step falls a little easier, and the next one a little easier yet. You then not only have momentum, but you also have direction. At this point, it doesn't matter so much which direction, as you can change it at any time. The important point is that you have *a* direction, where before you got over your inertia, you were directionless.

Trainee: Then does it get easier?

Tamarack: Yes and no. The threshold tends to hit those of us the hardest who are doing the best—precisely because it is only the most courageous who will have ventured the furthest out of our comfort zones and into our frontiers. Remember, though, that this same courage is also what makes them most prepared to handle the trials of the frontier.

Trainee: One more thing: How do I stay detached from the outcome once I have a direction?

Tamarack: By acknowledging the direction without attaching fear or hope to it. I've mentioned fear, but hope is another trap, another illusion of the mind to be aware of.

Trainee: Are you saying that hope is bad?

Tamarack: Let me respond this way: There is a saying that hope springs eternal, and spring eternal it must in order to entertain a future illusion. Yet when I listen to the Truth of those words, they're saying, *hope is an addiction*. We can never have the future: it is a false frontier: always out there, always beyond our grasp. Still, hope promises it to us—a promise it can never keep. Living in hope removes us from the Now, which is the only place we can experience our personal frontier and our Truth.

Here are important points to take away from this dialogue:

1. **Know that feelings of isolation and panic are normal** and expected in any major transition from old to new.What or who holds power over me?

2. **Seek support from others** on the journey to your personal frontier.

3. **Trust that you can reach your frontier.** Courage feeds itself: the more you show, the more you know.

4. **The journey is worth the effort.** You are worthy of becoming the communicator you know you can be.

This chapter concludes the guidance on listening. In the next section, we turn our attention to the roles of feelings and emotions in Truthspeaking.

The Chapter at a Glance

Opening our Hearts to Truth—and keeping them open—is a risk, and it takes great courage. Yet, there is no other way, as an open Heart without the courage to keep it open is like a bird without wings. The Truthlistening journey asks that we embrace the bitter as well as the sweet of what Truth brings. To pick and choose would be to live a False Truth.

The courage that Truthlistening requires is trust with risk: adventuring from the security of knowing to the frontier of the unknown. It is believing that we are capable of a better way of communicating. It is having faith in the fact that we are worthy of being happy and content with life.

When we live with this courage, we step out on our personal frontier: that realm where we find our Truth, inhabit the Now, and become finely attuned to the Web of Life. Entering the frontier requires letting go of our past and all that keeps us distanced from our Truth.

Re-becoming a Truthlistener is a life-changing experience. Leaving the old, familiar chitchat and pretense behind and getting down to the Heart of communication is fundamentally a journey of self-discovery.

On this journey, we may begin to rationalize abandoning the quest and finding contentment in things as they were. The mind can make abandoning the quest appear to be the quest itself. Yet deep down, we have this persistent, nagging sense that we are here in this life to realize our limits, then go beyond.

What we *perceive* as our limit is only the threshold between the known and the unknown. A river is a limit only because we haven't yet figured out a way to cross it. And it will remain a limit if we don't garner the courage to do so, or if we convince ourselves that we don't have the wherewithal to cross it.

As we let go of the past, we must also abandon the urge to seek *compatible relationships*. Although they are safe and comfortable, they are typically not very stimulating or growth-oriented. This is because we have chosen mirror images of ourselves, who only reinforce who we are (or at least our preferred illusion of self). *Complementary relationships,* on the other hand, stimulate and inspire.

At the start of every journey is inertia. The first step is the hardest because we need to translate potential energy into kinetic, to get our mass moving. The second step then falls a little easier, and the next one a little easier yet. We then not only have momentum, but we have direction, which is also difficult to initially establish.

When we venture forth overly cautious or fearful, we limit what we could potentially gain. When we use our past to chart our future, all we do is relive the past—we limit what our future could be by what our past has been. What we venture into is then only an illusion. If there is no risk, surprise, or unknown, it is not a frontier, and we will only find what is comfortable for us.

≋

PART THREE

THE ROLES OF FEELINGS AND EMOTIONS

My mate Lety was once told in a dream that her view of the world is only a perception. It doesn't become her reality until she feeds it emotionally. Right away when she related this to me, I felt the chill of awareness: as much as we pride ourselves in being creatures of reason, able to objectively observe and evaluate, we are actually feeling creatures. We continually alter our world, knowledge, and beliefs to accommodate our feelings.

In Chapter 8, we learned how our feelings fit into two groupings: core emotions and reactive feelings. Where feelings change likes clouds passing over the sun, our core emotions remain steady. In the following three chapters, we become intimately familiar with the personalities of feelings and emotions, along with learning how to use this knowledge in our relationships.

CHAPTER TEN

KNOWING OUR FEELINGS AND EMOTIONS

Our core emotions are central to our being. Reactive feelings act as warning signs that draw our attention to the need for emotional expression. They arise when we do not Truthspeak our core emotions. Reactive feelings then take over and assume the role of core emotions, displacing our Truth and aggravating our personal relationships.

Here are the core emotions, along with a sampling of the seemingly endless list of reactive feelings.

Core Emotions	Reactive Feelings	
Fear	Anger	Loneliness
Longing	Guilt	Despondency
	Sadness	Joy
	Stress	Excitement
	Envy	Jealousy
	Despair	Terror
	Anxiety	Panic
	Depression	Euphoria
	Hopelessness	Remorse

The core emotions: *fear* and *longing*, are intrinsic to all sentient life. They are seated in the old brain—the intuitive mind—and serve as pillars upon which every life experience rests. They protect and nourish us, while keeping us attuned to the rest of life. Without them, we would not exist. All reactive feelings are derivatives of the two core emotions.

The Essence of Our Core Emotions

Knowing fear and longing is essential to knowing and speaking our Truth. Let's take a look at each one as it relates to the human experience.

Fear is our protector. When we find ourselves on the threshold of a situation we may not be able to handle, we feel fear. It causes senses to sharpen and adrenaline to pump, in preparation for a fight-flight response. We fear only what we don't know (as in fear of the dark) or what overwhelms us (such as a threatening person).

Fear interrupts the state of bliss we naturally find ourselves in when we are fully aware and attuned. Here is where we are supposed to be; now is the best time to be here. Everything feels right with the world, whether or not we are happy or sad, hot or cold, hungry or full. The more we future project or dwell in the past, the more we are being guided by fear (see Chapter 12 for more on this).

Longing fuels our ever-present thirst for social contact. It is the glue that keeps us in relationship. The ground on which we walk, the air we breathe, the food we eat, the community of plants and animals of which we are part, the humans of our hearth, the dreams and ancient memories that guide us—we are in relationship with all of these.

Longing keeps us connected to the giving-receiving continuum which is life. We are here for one reason: to gift our beauty and uniqueness to our Relations. Giving is receiving, and neither can occur without the other. Yet we must give before we can receive, as giving creates the space for receiving. Reactive feelings surface when—for whatever reason—we quit giving.

The Core Emotions at a Glance

Fear is the lack of knowing. It keeps us in the now.
Longing keeps us seeking relationship. It is the reason for our ability to give.

THE HAPPINESS MYTH

Psychiatrist Thomas Szasz says, "Happiness is an imaginary condition, formerly attributed by the living to the dead, now usually attributed by adults to children, and by children to adults."[1] Our fixation on happiness was undoubtedly fueled by what may be the most famous phrase from the United States Declaration of Independence, which presents life, liberty, and the pursuit of happiness as inalienable rights.

I like to think that author Thomas Jefferson might have better expressed his intent by choosing the term joy instead of happiness. Think of happiness as secondary to joy: we can experience joy without happiness, but we cannot experience happiness without joy. When we are centered in our Heart-of-Hearts, we naturally dwell in the state of joy; so whether or not we are happy at the moment becomes a minor issue.

Differentiating Core Emotions and Reactive Feelings

Here is a story from the Zen tradition that shows a fundamental distinction.

Once there was a seeker who complained to an Elder, "Venerable sir, I have an uncontrollable temper: when anger wells up, I fly into a rage. What can I do to cure it?"

"You have something very rare," replied the Elder." I don't know that I have ever seen it. Please show it to me."

"I can't show it to you right now," said the seeker.

"When might you be able to?"

"It comes and goes without warning."

"Can it then be your true nature?" asked the Elder. "For if it were, you could bring it out any time. It appears, then, that you were not born with this temper, so it cannot be a part of you."[2]

When we are in Balance, which is being solidly seated in our core emotions, we experience no reactive feelings. This is our natural and intended state of being. This does not mean that reactive feelings are bad. There are no preferable or undesirable feelings—they all exist for a reason.

When we are in a state of core emotion, we have no need for concern. We are in touch with ourselves and the life around us, and we are taking care of things as they come up.

However, when we experience a reactive feeling, we are being told that we are out of Balance, i.e., running contrary to one or both of the core emotions. Anxiety results from not embracing fear, depression might follow our drifting out of balance with our core emotions, envy is often caused by not giving (an expression of Longing), and loneliness comes when we struggle in relationship (which is a tussle with Longing).

The long-term stress resulting from unresolved secondary feelings can be both physically and emotionally damaging—to ourselves and others. When I am not speaking my Truth, a backlog of feelings builds up. When I finally do speak my Truth, my Heart feels light; yet I am left with the muddiness of lingering feelings. This is because I have developed a relationship with them that is hard to break.

When I consistently speak my Truth in the moment, there is resolution and clarity, with no residual feelings or issues to deal with. I am free to honor the moment by living in my Truth and speaking it.

Sharing Emotions and Feelings

All emotions and feelings are legitimate in and of themselves and deserve to be shared—even reactive feelings. Verbalizing them accomplishes two things: it brings our attention to our reactive feelings, so that we can resolve them, and it makes others more aware of how we look and act in a particular emotional state. This helps them better intuit our feelings.

How to share feelings without triggering a reaction

First: Own the feeling. Express it as an "I feel..." statement, rather than "You make me feel...."

Second: State the core emotion before the reactive feeling, as in, "I've been feeling lonely lately, which made me jealous when you spent the afternoon with somebody else."

Here I state that I am feeling jealous not because my friend was out with someone else, but because I was feeling lonely. *My jealousy is secondary to my loneliness—my core Truth.* By expressing the secondary feeling within the cradle of the mother emotion, I allow the listener to hear my Truth without feeling blamed. This makes it much more likely that the listener will feel comfortable with my core emotion.

Reactive Feeling to Core Emotion Exercise

As Truthlisteners, we know that just as Truth lies beneath feelings, core emotions lie beneath reactive feelings. When we want to fully speak our Truths, we need to voice both the reactive feelings and core emotions. Here is how to do it:

Reactive Feeling	Core Emotion	Both Expressed
"I'm mad at you for not waking me up."	Fear	"I'm angry because I'm late for work and my boss is going to chew me out."
"I'm feeling anxious about tonight."	Longing	"I get a queasy feeling whenever I go on a date."
"I'm glad we're going out together."	Fear and Longing	"I was afraid I'd be alone tonight, and now I'm happy, because I feel wanted."

Now perform this exercise

1. **List six secondary feelings** that you have experienced over the past few days.
2. **Note the core emotions** behind them.
3. **Combine the two**, in order to fully express your Truth.

117

BE SPECIFIC

Some terms associated with feeling, such as love and upset, have become so overused that they have lost their character. They have taken on nondescript, generic meanings that allow them to be attached to nearly anything. We can love God, and we can love that new Pepsi commercial. Rather than using love, I express the quality and texture of my feeling: what I find special about her, how she inspires me, and the range of feelings that fill me when we are together. The same with upset; I want the person to know what I am actually feeling, whether it be anger, frustration, jealousy, stress, anxiety, vengeance, or disappointment.

The Feeling Fallacy

I have counseled a number of people who were confused about what a feeling is and how to clearly express it. We commonly hear "I feel hungry," which is a primal urge, not a feeling. "I feel that you want to leave," is really an observation, and "I feel disrespected" is a judgment.

Statements that begin with "I feel that you" or "You make me feel" might express a feeling, yet in essence they are externalizations. We are either crediting or blaming someone else for our feelings, when in fact no one can make us feel anything. We feel as we do because of who we are, where we've come from, and what we've experienced. Even a seemingly innocent statement like, "When you cry, I get sad" can be an externalization.

The commonly used "I feel that you..." has nothing to do with feeling. It is either a judgment of your feelings or a projection of my feelings onto you. Even if I could state what you were feeling, it would hardly be speaking my Truth. And even more importantly, it is not for me to speak your Truth.

An often-used variation is *I feel* followed with a participle (a verb ending in *ed*), as in *I feel lied to, I feel cheated*, or *I feel ignored*. Even though the statement starts with *I*, the *ed* makes it a *you* statement. Rather than expressing our feelings, these statements are judgments—or at best, opinions or assumptions. Instead of expressing our Heart-Voices, we are letting our victimized egos speak.

A Quick Way to Identify Actual Feelings

- If it's *fear* or *longing*, it *is* a feeling (or more specifically, a *core emotion*).
- If it's *glad, sad, mad,* or any variation thereof, it *is* a feeling (more specifically, a *reactive feeling*). For examples of variations, see the *Reactive Feelings* list several pages back.
- Anything else is either a projection or a cover-up.

The Danger of Words

With our word-based culture, we still find it hard to share our feelings. In large part, it is because *sharing a feeling* has come to mean that we are expected to come up with words to describe the feeling as closely as possible. People make careers out of talking, singing, and writing about feelings—and in the process it appears that we have forgotten to simply feel them.

In addition, word-based communication has intrinsic shortcomings:

- It necessitates a shared reality, where the sharing of feeling honors individual reality.
- Words are merely symbols—approximations—for what we want to convey. Words, then, tend to depersonalize feelings.
- It's easy to forget that words are not the feeling; they can only help in sharing the feeling.
- Verbiage can convey only the surface, rational aspect of feeling.
- Words draw their meaning from association with past experience, where feeling is here and now.

These points seem to indicate that we would be wise in choosing feeling-related wording carefully and using it sparsely.

THE WORD MASK

Have you ever taken advantage of words' ability to dance around a feeling by using them to deliberately mask or misrepresent it? The reason it works is that:

- *We are more accustomed to describing a feeling than to connecting directly with it.*
- *We have forgotten that body language is intrinsically honest.*
- *and that Authentic feeling exists irrespective of verbal diversion.*

The Wolves I lived with communicated a broad range of feelings with the aid of only a few basic sounds. Their emotional sharing was so effective and honest because it transcended the narrow band of sound and encompassed the whole spectrum of communication. I had to be sensitive to every nuance of their movements and psychic energies—and to my intuitive impressions and ego filters—in order to fully read their feelings.

I find the same with my fellow humans. When I ask someone to describe his most profound emotional experience, he'll usually recall an event that was intensely kinetic and largely nonverbal. This is typical for us, as research confirms that after a few seconds we may forget the words associated with an emotional experience yet the emotional memory can last a lifetime.[3]

Feeling is *now* and body language is *now*, which means Truthspeaking is *now*. When we are in the Now, feeling emanates from us as clearly as does the warmth and crackle of a campfire. At the same time, we are just as capable of clearly sensing the feelings of others who are in the Now.

This is true emotional health—the lean, clean, and immediate flow of feelings and Truth. It leaves no pent-up or reactive feeling in its wake, and therefore no frustration, depression, or loss of self-esteem. Each moment, each sharing, cleanses itself.

One Step at a Time

At this point, it may be good for us to be reminded that verbal communication is not intrinsically bad. Look at it this way: Words can help express feeling—if they are few and well-chosen. Trying to share a feeling largely with words is like viewing a photo of a river and calling it a canoe trip.

Imagine your whole life being like those precious moments you feel with somebody when you allow your feelings to freely flow. This is the way of all living things—even us humans—when we allow ourselves to function as we evolved, which is using nonverbal communication as our first language. After all, we are genetically programmed for it. If we allowed and encouraged it, perhaps those blissful nonverbal moments could flower into a blissful life.

Getting there involves being able to move beyond words to communicate our feelings. Yet words can serve as a stepping-stone. Expressing our feelings clearly and succinctly with words can help those close to us to gradually become familiar with our personal style of sensory expressiveness. Over time, we can then pare down the verbal component.

Improving Nonverbal Fluency

Sensory communication can be as precise and as rich as verbal. Facial expression, body language, tone of voice, posture, and rate of breathing are cues that we pick up directly, along with indirect cues from how the "speaker" is affecting the immediate environment.

If I say "I'm angry," that seems clear enough. However, I may be only mildly irritated, or I could be doing a good job of controlling my rage and deliberately down-playing it. Yet if my fists and jaw are clenched, the veins in my forehead are bulging, and I'm hissing through my teeth, you know precisely how I am feeling, no matter what I say or don't say. This is direct, sensory communication.

Now let's repeat the reactive feeling to core emotion exercise from a few pages back, this time doing it nonverbally:

Reactive Feeling, Nonverbal	Core Emotion	Both Expressed Nonverbally
"~~I'm mad at you for not getting me up.~~" A glance at the alarm clock, followed by a frown and a cold stare.	Fear	"~~I'm angry because I'm late for work and~~ ~~My boss is going to chew me out.~~" A huff and a downcast, defeated look while scurrying out the door.
"~~I'm feeling anxious about tonight.~~" A pensive look while trying to decide on what to wear.	Longing	"~~I get a queasy feeling whenever I go on a date.~~" Holding your stomach while you go and get something to settle it.

Follow this by doing the same with the six reactive feeling-core emotion experiences you listed.

Beware of False Mirroring

The more attuned we become to our feelings, the more we must be careful about adopting them as our functioning platform, rather than our Heart-of-Hearts. When we allow our feelings to guide us in relationship, it is as though we hold a mirror to the face of the person.

This is different from the type of mirroring we might do while Truthlistening, where we restate what we have heard, for the purpose of clarification. With feeling mirroring, we end up simply reflecting back feelings, rather than listening from the Heart, then speaking our Truth. In other words, we react emotionally.

In doing so, we stay safe behind our mirror. We have risked nothing, yet neither have we gained anything—other than a stale relationship.

Imagine being with a group of people, with all of them holding out-turned mirrors in front of them. When a statement comes your way, you hold up your mirror and reflect it back at the group, and everyone else does the same. Neither Truthspeaking nor Truthlistening occurs, because without an open Heart to receive Truth, it cannot be heard. It's as if it that Truth had never been spoken.

Here are some of the reasons that such situations evolve:

- We have an innate capacity for being in trusting relationship with only fifteen to twenty-five people, and most of us are involved with many more than that in our daily lives. Overextending ourselves in this way compromises our ability to do much more than mirroring back what others share with us.

- "The dysfunctional family" has become a cultural icon. Rather than working to improve our emotional communication, we celebrate the very dysfunction that hurts us.[4]

- Many of us do not know ourselves well enough to speak or listen from our Heart-of-Hearts.

As a result, we react—i.e. hold up a mirror—instead of enact. It's no wonder that so many of us feel unfulfilled in our relationships and would rather listen to music or interact with screen images than with people.

The Chapter at a Glance

We have core emotions and reactive feelings. The core emotions: *fear* (which is essentially lack of knowing) and *longing* (which prompts us to seek relationship), are intrinsic to all sentient life. They are seated in the old brain—the intuitive mind—and serve as the pillars upon which every life experience rests.

Our reactive feelings act as warning signs. They arise when we do not Truthspeak or act upon our core emotions. Anxiety, a reactive feeling, could result from not embracing fear; and loneliness can arise from the longing inherent in a dysfunctional relationship.

When we are in Balance—fully grounded in our core emotions—we experience no reactive feelings. This is our natural and intended state of being. Yet it would be imprecise to then assume that reactive feelings are bad. There are no preferable or undesirable feelings. They all exist for a reason and deserve to be shared—even reactive feelings.

One way to share these feelings without triggering a reaction in the listener is to:

1. **Own the feeling.** Express it as "I feel…" rather than "You make me feel…."

2. **State the core feeling before the secondary feeling.** "I've been feeling lonely, and so I felt jealous that you were out with others."

When we express the secondary feeling within the cradle of the mother feeling, we allow the listener to hear our Truth *without feeling blamed.* This makes it much more likely that the other person will empathize with our core emotion.

Statements beginning with "I feel that you…"or "You make me feel…" followed by a participle (a verb that ends in *ed,* as in *lied to* and *ignored*) might express a feeling, yet in essence we are blaming someone else for our feelings. Besides the fact that no one can make us feel anything, these statements are often judgments. At best, they are opinions or assumptions.

In our culture, sharing your feelings has come to mean something other than literally sharing feelings. I'm expected to come up with words to describe a feeling as closely as possible. Yet, words are merely symbols—approximations—for what we want to convey. Remember: words cannot convey feeling; they can only crudely describe it.

As with reactive feelings, verbal communication is not bad. There simply exists a better way for emotional sharing. As we continue to express our core emotions and reactive feelings clearly and succinctly, those close to us will become more and more familiar with our nonverbal forms of emotional expression. As this occurs, we can gradually reduce our verbiage.

Nonverbal communication is conveyed by facial expression, body language, tone of voice, posture, rate of breathing, intuitive impulse, and indirectly from effects on the surrounding environment. Nonverbal sharing can be as precise and rich as word-based expression.

Feeling is *now* and body language is *now*, which means Truthspeaking is *now*. When we are in the Now, feeling emanates from us as clearly as does the warmth and crackle of a campfire.

Chapter Ten Endnotes

1   Thomas Szasz, *The Second Sin* (New York: Anchor Press, 1973), 36.

2   http://tuvienquangduc.com.au/English/story/01zenstory61-80.html#75.%20Temper

3   J.E. Le Doux, L. Romanski, and A. Xagoraris, "Indelibility of Subcortical Emotional Memories," *Journal of Cognitive Neuroscience* 1 (1991): 238-43.

4   Sharon Jayson, "Thanksgiving: A Time to Celebrate Family Dysfunction?" *USA Today*, last modified November 2013, accessed 20 April 2019, http://www.usatoday.com/story/news/nation/2013/11/24/family-dysfunctional-thanksgiving/3618435/.

CHAPTER ELEVEN

ANGER REFLUX

Not long ago, a young girl named Blue-Feather was being tormented by Wolverine (her people's term for *anger*), because her younger brother could dive deeper down in the Lake than she could.

A Wolverine lives inside each of us. When we become angry, Wolverine awakens. We can go a long time without knowing he is there, because he is small and prefers to sleep above anything else.

Wolverine is known by another name—Skunk-Bear. When his sleep is disturbed, he can be as vile as an irritated Skunk and as ill-tempered as a wounded Bear. He may be small enough to fit inside you, yet when he is awakened he can be ornery and famished enough to devour you.

"Father," said Blue-Feather to Wanders-the-River, "Wolverine has been roused inside me, and he has sprayed my eyes with his putrid musk. I can no longer see clearly. And he rips and tears at my Heart with his terrible claws. I cannot think clearly or trust my feelings. He is greedy—he is swallowing all of my insides. I am afraid!"

Blue-Feather loved and trusted Wanders-the-River. He was a good hunter and honored Guardian of his People. Although he was her uncle, she called him "father" because that was the way of her People. Aunts and uncles are often just as closely involved in raising the children as are parents.

"Daughter," responded Wanders-the-River, "I would like to tell you the story of when I was about your age. I was training to become a Guardian, and I would sometimes compare myself with others. When I thought I did not match up, I would sometimes feel Wolverine waking. When I got frustrated because of my lack of ability, Wolverine would growl and churn my stomach. If I did not feed him, he would feed on me. Before I knew it, Wolverine had consumed me—I became Wolverine."

"Oh no, father! What happened to you?"

"I grew scared, my daughter, just as you are now. I had a wise uncle, so I went to him, and this is what he told me: 'When Wolverine awakens, it is because he is hungry. You must feed him, because if you do not, he will eat your insides."

"But Father, I do not want to feed him—he is nothing but an angry, smelly little Bear!"

"Blue-Feather, you do not respect him; that is why he tears at your Heart. If you do feed him, you can choose his food. Welcome him as you would a respected guest at a Feast. Tell him you would be honored if he would sit with you and share his teachings. Then feed him your presence and your gratitude, and he will grow content and fall back asleep.'"

"Thank you, Father; I now see the teaching that Wolverine brings me. He is much more than a mad Bear. He rumbles and grumbles for a reason—so that I will listen to him."

This traditionally based story came to me one day when I was reflecting on how anger has a life of its own. The inspiration came from my clan sister, Gegekwe, and this telling is in her honor.

Looking Deeper

Buddhist sage Thich Nhat Hanh suggests that we sit with our anger as we would with a crying baby: giving comfort and listening.[1] If we are attentive, the baby will tell us what she needs, and so will our anger.

Because of anger's intensity, we often take it to be a core emotion, rather than a reactive feeling pointing *toward* a core emotion. When we listen deeply and honestly to anger, it usually tells us what the real issue is. This Truth (which is typically fear or shades of longing, such as sorrow or insecurity) is what would most likely be expressed instead of anger if we were able to Truthspeak.

Anger, like fear or pain, exists to give warning. Yet there is a distinct difference between the effect of anger on others and the effect of core emotions. This is why anger is referred to as a *reactive* feeling. We can discover this by bringing our Truthlistening skills into play:

First: Acknowledge your anger. This creates the opening for listening.

Second: Listen closely for what at first seems to have no voice. Yet if you are Truthlistening, you will hear it cry out.

Take the case of someone who expresses anger, which immediately triggers a defensive response. Yet the deeper Truth is that the anger elicited fear. Only the fear went unrecognized because it was masked by the overriding defensive response.

On the other hand, the direct expression of a core emotion such as fear seldom results in defensiveness and masked feelings. That allows the more normal response from others of presence, openness, and empathy.

The Faces of Anger

When we Truthspeak our anger and discern its root cause, we fully honor it. However, when we hold onto anger or allow it to transform into rage, it becomes problematic. There are two types of problematic anger:

1. **Incendiary**: the instant adrenaline-fueled, face-reddening flare-up that overwhelms us. It often results from being shamed, threatened, or having our fight-flight response triggered in some other way.
2. **Simmering**: the long-term anger that often has a rational component. We feed it by stewing over it, which creates a chronic condition that casts a shadow over much of what we say and do.

Anger develops a life of its own and will keep burning as long as it has something to feed upon. Traditional Hawaiians acknowledge this with their saying, A'ole e 'ōlelo mai ana ke ahi ua ana ia: *Fire will never say that it has had enough.*[2]

When we allow the fire to burn, it becomes the pure, unleashed feeling we call *rage*. Here are the distinguishing characteristics of anger and rage:

Anger	Rage
Typically accompanied by externalizing, blaming, and justifications or denial.	Incoherent.
Can be guided, controlled, redirected, or transformed.	Unstoppable.
Its direction and intensity can be affected by others.	Blind to its surroundings, blind to Truth.

Simmering anger dishonors the core nature of anger, which is that it self-eliminates. When we experience anger, we also feel an intense urge to get rid of it.[3] It is as though we were intuitively attempting to follow the guidance of the Buddha, who said that when we hold onto anger it is like grabbing a hot coal to throw at someone, only we are the ones who get burned.

Everything exists for a reason. We have been discussing the hurtful aspects of anger, while at the same time it brings us gifts:

- **It is unsettling.** This motivates us to address unmet needs, which releases the anger.
- **It is fragile.** More than any other reactive feeling, it quickly diminishes when we take responsibility for it and hold ourselves accountable.[4]
- **It promotes confrontation,** which creates the opportunity to share and release it.[5]

Why We Misread Anger

Next to the fear of not being accepted, fear of anger is the most common reason people give me for not Truthspeaking. Many of us have been taught that anger is a feeling to be ashamed of. Some of us have been punished for getting angry. In response, so many of us have learned to pretend that we are not angry. Yet it is still there, screaming for release. The upshot is that we have become inept at expressing anger, so we distance ourselves from those we care for.

Yet that is not the only response to anger: some of us have learned to use it as a way to be heard. We see it as effective communication, so we automatically resort to it, often when it is not needed.

This so easily creates over-reactive situations. In order to survive them, we typically become hypersensitive, aggressive or judgmental. (These are self-protective boundaries, which— unfortunately—also impose distance between ourselves and those we care for.)

Others choose more culturally-accepted displacement/ avoidance behaviors, such as aggressive dance, music, movies, video games, reading materials, or sports. Still others turn to psychotherapy or religious practice. Many of us end up being haunted by violent dreams and fantasies.

Often, then, the only people we can feel comfortable with are passive, apologetic enablers. This is because we tend to avoid people who challenge us when we are afflicted with chronic anger. Instead, we gravitate toward those who tolerate our outbursts—and perhaps even take responsibility for them.

When none of this works—and it seldom does for long—the anger builds up to the point where we can't help but express it. Only by this point all we can do is vent it as rage. We have lost touch with the Truth: the feelings and thoughts behind our anger. Others, as well, are bound to misread us.

Finding the Truth in Our Anger

The metaphor of *venting* our anger is powerful. It is also ineffective. Let's look more closely at this: we generally consider the venting of anger to be healthy, because if it is not released, it will either build up and explode or fester inside and cause other ills.

As rationally sound as this argument appears to be, simple venting does not bring us closer to our Truth. Nor can it re-center us, as the venting process is still anger-based.

When we continually use venting as a way of dealing with anger, we set up a pattern that ends up encouraging anger. By venting, we gain the pleasure of emotional expression, and we are being heard. These uplifting and necessary outcomes make it appear that venting is a helpful technique, so we end up unconsciously conditioning ourselves to turn to anger in order to be recognized and feel emotionally fulfilled.

Anger is energy, and energy is flow: it has source and direction. By allowing the flow, as in *venting anger*, we do not necessarily recognize or honor our anger's source and direction. Instead, we become passive channels of the flow: pawns of the source and blind to the direction.

Imagine venting steam from a boiler which has built up too much pressure. We save the moment, yet in continuing to vent steam, we perpetuate a potentially explosive boiler situation. It seems as though we are doing the right thing, yet over time we become frustrated and dismayed, as there is no fundamental change. The same is true with anger: it keeps surfacing, even though we we're doing the "right" thing with it.

When we know the source of our anger, we can direct its flow, so that we are not blowing the energy into the air, but rather going to its source, so that we can restore centeredness.

If for whatever reason going to the source turns out to be impossible (such as in cases of trauma or severe depression), we can redirect the flow of energy to carry us beyond the realm of the source. When there is movement, there is the potential for change.

This is not expressing anger, but rather accepting it as a gift, then grasping it as a tool for returning to centeredness. Following is an effective way to use the anger tool.

Truth-in-Anger Exercise

When you say or think this	Ask yourself:
"I'm shouting because I am angry."	"Why do I feel that I am not being heard?"
"Why am I always angry?"	"What is the root of this habit?"
"Why does he always make me angry?"	"Why do I feel the need to create distance between him and me?"
"Why do I use an angry tone with her?"	"How am I feeling challenged by her?"
"I gave in to him because he got angry."	"Why am I afraid of anger being expressed?"
"I suppress my angry feelings."	"Why am I ashamed of my anger?"
"I'm angry because I hurt myself."	"Do I need to take responsibility for my actions?"
"I'm angry because I'm late," or, "I'm angry because I didn't get this job finished on time."	"What unrealistic expectations do I (or someone else) have of myself?"
I forgot why I got angry."	"What feeling did I not express before I got angry?"

Transforming Anger

Asking ourselves the above questions helps uncover our core emotion, rather than merely blowing off some reactive feeling.

This legend from the Nama Hottentot people of southwest Africa illustrates the folly of acting reactively:

> *Not too long ago, a young shepherd was out herding his sheep. The afternoon was hot, and he sat down to rest in the shade of a tree. Before long, he nodded off.*
>
> *The lead ram, who was grazing nearby, saw the shepherd's lowered head and took it as a threat to his position. The ram charged the shepherd and gave him a good butt.*
>
> *Tumbling over, the shepherd jumped up in anger, tackled the ram, and threw him off of the nearby cliff. The flock, seeing their leader disappear over the rim, followed him to their deaths.*
>
> *The shepherd, mad with grief, wailed, "What a fool I am— look what my senseless anger has done!"*

The shepherd has come to an awareness; now how can he transform his reactiveness?

First: recognize that destructive reactiveness is an insidious learned behavioral pattern.

Second: look to its source.

Third: create a nondestructive response pattern.

It may sound simple, but that doesn't necessarily make it easy. The reason is that flashes of anger catch us by surprise, so we are not prepared for them. Being creatures of habit and pattern, we automatically resort to what we have always done.

Yet this is not a limiting factor—we can prepare ourselves to respond differently. This transforms anger, a reactive feeling, into a feeling of choice. It works like this:

Scenario one: I trip on a rock. Accustomed to disowning my actions, I blame the rock for being there on the trail and angrily curse it.

Scenario two: I have been practicing taking responsibility for my actions, so I realize right away that I tripped because I wasn't observant. I take it as a lesson for becoming a better hiker.

Sharing Anger

For me, taking responsibility for my anger includes considering the guidance of my Elders:

The best time to deal with pain and anger is now.

When there are others involved, I am to take my feelings to them and ask if they will claim their part.

Here is the method I was given to use when sharing anger with others who were involved:

- **Own the feeling.** *All* feelings deserve to be acknowledged and honored. We must remember, though, that *we are the cause of our feelings—no one can force us to feel one way or another.*

- **Share the core emotion and the reactive feeling**. Voicing our anger alongside the core emotion honors both, while allowing the listener to listen and empathize where it fits for him.

- **Thank him.** While it may seem strange, we thank the other person because he has pushed the button that gave us the opportunity to discover why we reacted with anger—the key to our healing.

In summary, anger is not something to be afraid of or feel shame over. It is an invaluable guide to our Inner Wisdom. The Honor Way with anger is to listen carefully to what anger has to say; then thank it, bless it, and send it on its way. Only then, as Wanders-the-River from the chapter-opening story shared, will Wolverine grow content and fall back asleep. Only then are we ready to speak the Truth of our Heart with clarity and calm.

The Chapter at a Glance

In this chapter, we learned to recognize anger as a gift: a counselor and guide to Wisdom. Buddhist sage Thich Nhat Hanh suggests that we sit with our anger and be comforting and lis-ten, as we would with a crying baby.[6] In this way, she tells us what she needs, and so does our anger.

We often misread anger by seeing it as a core emotion, rather than as a reactive feeling pointing us *to* the core emotion. When we can do this, we usually discover deep-seated feelings of fear, sorrow, or insecurity.

Next to fear of not being accepted, fear of anger is the most common reason we give for not Truthspeaking. This is the fall-out of using anger to be heard, which many of us have learned to do. This creates an over-reactive dynamic, to which some people respond by becoming hypersensitive, aggressive or judgmental.

Simultaneously, our culture tells us that anger is a feeling to be ashamed of. Some of us have been punished for getting angry, so we have learned to pretend that we are not. Yet the anger persists and screams for release. To cope, some of us have distanced ourselves from those we care for, rather than risk becoming angry.

The Elders have told me that the best time to deal with anger is *now*, and the best way is to take it to others who might be involved, asking if they will claim their part. Yet effectively deal-ing with anger involves more than simply venting it. If this is all we do, we merely become passive channels of the flow. We remain pawns to our anger and blind to its deeper source.

To find this deeper source, we must turn to our Truthlistening skills. We will then be able to identify the voiceless emotion than our anger masks. As well, we may become sensitive to the fear that is elicited in others when someone becomes angry.

Where anger triggers defensiveness, expressions of core emotions generally do not. We have no reason to shield our-selves from a creature who is fearful, hurt, or confused. Rather, we are drawn to respond with empathy.

When someone triggers anger in us, we can respond in this way: *first*, acknowledge and own the feeling; *second*, share both the feeling and the core emotion; and *third*, thank the person for pushing the button which gives us the opportunity to connect with the deeper reason for our anger—and which gives us the opportunity to heal.

Anger is not something to fear or be ashamed of. It typically becomes problematic only when we repress it or let it transform into rage. We honor both the feeling and ourselves when we Truthspeak our anger and discern its root cause.

Chapter Eleven Endnotes

1   Thich Nhat Hanh, *Taming the Tiger Within: Meditations on Transforming Difficult Emotions* (Penguin, 2004), 57.

2   Mary Kawena Pukui, *ʻŌlelo Noʻeau, Hawaiian Proverbs and Poetical Sayings*, 26.

3   Stefan Stürmer and Bernd Simon, "Pathways to Collective Protest: Calculation, Identification, or Emotion? A Critical Analysis of the Role of Group-Based Anger in Social Movement Participation," *Journal of Social Issues* 65, no. 4 (2009): 703.

4   Cendri A. Hutcherson and James J. Gross, "The Moral Emotions: A Social–Functionalist Account of Anger, Disgust, and Contempt." *Journal of Personality and Social Psychology* 100, no. 4 (2011): 720.

5   Emma F. Thomas, Craig McGarty, and Kenneth I. Mavor, "Transforming 'Apathy Into Movement': The Role of Prosocial Emotions in Motivating Action for Social Change." *Personality and Social Psychology Review* 13, no. 4 (2009): 323.

6   Thich Nhat Hanh, *Taming the Tiger Within: Meditations on Transforming Difficult Emotions*, 57.

CHAPTER TWELVE

LIFE ACCORDING TO FEAR

Much like Wolverine in the last chapter's story, Fear tears at our Hearts and hijacks our Truth if we ignore or overindulge it. When we welcome Fear as we would a respected guest to a Feast, then feed him our presence and gratitude, we can hear what he has to teach us—without being overpowered to the point of undermining our Truths.

Think of Fear as a Pony galloping across the prairie. Our lot is to ride the Pony, yet we have the choice of either being dragged under her belly or sitting up on her back. The prairie—our life— looks quite different when we are flopping around in the dust with sharp hooves pounding around us, as opposed to guiding the Pony with a full view of the prairie and the wind blowing through our hair.

We choose whether Fear will counsel or trample us. This chapter gives assurance that Fear is a welcome companion on our return to Truth. We typically hear the opposite: that Fear is our worst enemy and our only limitation. However, it is our attachment to these beliefs, rather than Fear itself, that makes it destructive.

Here are four fundamental ways that Fear serves as our benefactor:

1. **It acts as a mirror,** to help us see our stripped-down, unadorned selves.
2. **It shows what we need to learn** and become aware of.
3. **It keeps us safe,** telling us where to stop and turn.
4. **It is a loyal friend,** always there for us when needed.

The negative perception of Fear dominates because modern civilization is scarcity based. Our way of life separates us from the natural abundance: what many Native people call the *gifting way.* As a result, we live in fear of not having enough, of never being good enough. We are wired to live lives of cooperation and caring, yet we grow up being taught disconnection and competitiveness. This creates the illusion that if we can only win, we'll have achieved a fear-free existence.

Fear is a core emotion, which means that we cannot will it away. Trying to do so only makes it persist and reappear in one of its many shades: anxiety, panic, envy, aggressiveness, jealousy, competitiveness, resignation, depression, feelings of inadequacy, and various forms of self-abuse.

When we embrace Fear as part of the human experience, we can begin to discern the Truth it has to share. By not surrendering to the emotion, we can stay on the Pony even when she speeds up. In honoring Fear this way, we honor ourselves.

How to Honor Fear

Some people construe reactive emotional responses such as anger, jealousy, and Fear as negative. However, they are an integral part of who we are. Without them, we would have been long dead, as they form the guideposts for our safe functioning.

Notice that I said *guideposts* rather than *barriers*. Where guideposts keep us from stumbling blindly along in the emotional wilderness, barriers would never allow us to reach it—and to reach it is essential, as this is where life becomes an adventure of self-discovery. Where barriers are absolute, guideposts provide awareness, sensitivity, and the voice of wisdom.

Fear is no more or less than a lack of knowing. When we hear noises in the night, we typically imagine them to be coming from the biggest, meanest possible source. This is a healthy and necessary survival response, to prepare us for worst-case scenarios. Yet this also results in some of us fearing the night, rather than the unknowns it holds.

Here's how well-functioning Fear works:

First: It magnifies our perception of a threat to our welfare.

Second: It motivates us to get ready for the most extreme possibility.

Third: The process reveals the source of our Fear.

In this way, Fear becomes our guide. When we get accustomed to working with Fear, we'll be able to not only enter the darkness, but be quite comfortable with it.

How to Make Fear Your Guide

1. **Identify your Fear** by giving it a descriptive name that shows its character.
2. **Envision your Fear** by imagining that you are walking into it. What does it feel like? Who and what do you meet? How long can you stand to be there?
3. **Leave the place of Fear**, but do it alone, in privacy and security.
4. **List who and what you met** there that distressed you, and accept them as gifts from your Fear.
5. **Open each gift** and get to know it.

Here is the story of someone who used this method:

"My friend fear's name is Creepy Bugsie, and the gifts he has given me are Spiders, Worms, and Slugs. I took those gifts one at a time, starting with Spiders. I got a video on Spiders at the library, along with a field guide and a book of stories about Spiders. Through them I've come to know that most of my fears about Spiders are unfounded: poisonous Spider bites in my area are very rare, and knowing the Spiders' habits and preferred habitat will keep me out of harm's way.

"I've learned that Pholcidae (which we usually refer to as Daddy Longlegs or cellar spiders) is one of the most poisonous Spiders, but actually has mouth parts too small to bite a Human. To my surprise, I discovered that he and other Spiders

are actually quite beneficial, as they eat untold numbers of insects, some of which are harmful to us. I now understand that there are Spiders in my basement because there are insects there that they control. If there were no insects, there would be no Spiders, as they wouldn't be able to survive.

"All that was well and good, but I still found myself squeamish around Spiders. So I visited a nearby nature center, where the naturalist offered to take me on a walk to see Spiders in their natural habitat. I was amazed at how beautiful some of them were, and how industrious, and how devoted to their young. And they were quite unconcerned about me—not one of them lunged at me or tried to crawl into my hair!

"Now for the true test. The naturalist had a friend who had pet Tarantulas. He offered to contact her and ask if I might come over for a visit. Even though my chest tightened and my palms got cold and clammy, I agreed. I knew that this was the ultimate facing of my fear, and I trusted in the process.

"After that Tarantula, named Mousey, walked down my arm and perched on my hand, I was ready to concede not only to an attitude adjustment about Spiders, but to a potential new world opening before me. I couldn't imagine Tarantulas instead of my cuddly Cats, but I could see the potential for my phobia over other creepy-crawlies melting away as well."

When we learn to embrace Fear, we broaden our perspectives. We move from unknowing to knowing. Many of our Fears go far beyond Spiders—to the point that they structure our worldviews. This is so ubiquitous that we find ourselves living in a culture starved for Truth, yet rich with all types of Fear.

We each share the essence of all these Fears. In other words, *fear is fear*. The contexts, triggers, and outcomes may be distinct, yet the Fear itself is the same. This is a godsend, as all the various and seemingly diverse types of Fear can be befriended using the one method I just shared.

When we enter the unknown walking *with* our Fear, we can recognize our limits without being held back by our perceived limitations. In exploring my acrophobia with Fear as my guide, I found my edge, and I am content with that. My acrophobia is no longer a limitation, as I can now fully function at heights within my comfort zone without being paralyzed by what might happen if I pushed myself just one step higher.

WHEN FEAR TAKES ON ITS OWN LIFE

The approach to fear mitigation presented here may not help in cases where chronic fear has created a catatonic state of stress. Resulting secondary fears, disconnectedness, and denial can mask the initial fear to the point where it is no longer recognizable. Here we go beyond the scope of this chapter; please consult my book Breaking the Trauma Code *and/or seek professional guidance.*

How We Dishonor Fear

The antidote to Fear is not fearlessness. That is denial of another sort, as it insulates us from our Fear by trying to silence it. Plain and simple, fearlessness is foolishness. The fearless one is the bold one, the risk-taker, the undaunted optimist, the tireless extrovert. Inside—and unsuspecting to most—one typically finds a trembling, lonely person.

On the other hand, overindulging Fear can morph it into paranoia. I know a woman who lives in such terror of her surroundings that she maintains tight control of nearly everything in her grasp: her children, her possessions, her feelings. She is consumed by a conspiracy theory that supports her belief that whatever is beyond her control is a threat. She may be the saddest woman I've met, for she knows her limitations but not her limits.

People like her have surrendered to their limitations by building a wall between themselves and the dark. They then live as if the darkness does not exist. In doing so:

- **They live without love in its fullness,** for love ventures into the dark.

- **They live without inquisitiveness,** for inquisitiveness is a calling from the dark.

- **They continue life without coming to know themselves,** as they have abandoned their personal frontier.

This last point is most tragic. I learned about it first hand when I was a young adult. Fear's shadow would pass my door, and I would give him as much attention as I would a fleeting cloud passing over the sun. Yet I felt the chill, which I denied as well by drawing closer to the fire.

Yet the shadow would return, as though he were haunting me. Each time, he seemed bigger and gruffer than the time before. His voice rumbled so deeply in his chest that I could no longer make it out. Even worse, I could barely hear myself beneath his growl. It got to the point where I sank into depression and could barely function in the constant chill of his shadow.

One day in utter desperation, I somehow mounted a super-human effort to open that door and embrace him. Immediately, I sank into the deepest depression I'd ever known. I taunted suicide. Yet I wouldn't go back. My struggle to keep the door open leached so much vital energy that I was left physically debilitated for months afterward. I didn't have the strength to stand upright for any period of time, I had trouble digesting food, and I was developing an ulcer. I would cry over the smallest disturbance. On top of that, it cost me my wife and my business.

Yet I lived through it. With nothing left to lose, I was now able to crawl before my Fear without pretext or delusion. I sat there, and he gently touched my shoulder. It turned out that all he wanted was for me to sit with him and listen.

He now knows that my door is always open, so he comes as a friend and speaks his Truth in a manner that is easy for me to understand and accept.

Fear of Growing

To embrace Fear, we must confront our apprehension of what Fear might hold. When we go out into the night woods with a flashlight, we learn not about the night, but about light. Rather than embracing the dark, we are only looking into it from the perspective of light. This keeps the dark at a distance.

When we walk in the dark, we develop eyes for the dark. We then discover that there is light within the dark. No longer is the dark something distant and frightful; now we can come to know the Truth it holds.

The dark is a metaphor for our unknowing, and the light represents the familiar. Approaching the unknown with the familiar keeps us in ignorance; i.e., in a state of Fear.

Forty years ago, I heard a woman named Wabun Wind (partner of Makwa Giizis, one of my Elders) speak these words, and I have never forgotten them: "We can't grow until we quit clinging to Fear. We are afraid to open ourselves to change because we haven't tasted the beauty and gentleness that will come. We are afraid to change because we don't yet know that change is possible. Like all of us, we cling to the old just because it is familiar."

Fear comes to us for one primary reason: to tell its story. Though Fear can first loom as a raging monster, he gets smaller and gentler the more we let him in.

What Fear helps us do through story:

- **Proceed** cautiously.
- **Look** at all angles.
- **Consider** possible harm to self and others.
- **Prepare** adequately.
- **Think** before acting.

When we can hear these Truths in our Fear's stories, we recognize Fear as honored counsel to our Heart-of-Hearts. Once Fear has served, we can bless it and send it on its way.

The Costs of Chronic Fear

Experiencing Fear is intended to be temporary, as it is mainly an awareness tool and catalyst for change. Think of it as a doorway to our potential. Like holding onto Anger, when we let Fear linger, it ends up hurting rather than helping. Here are just four of the ways it does so:

1. **It causes cognitive distortions:** irrational or exaggerated thoughts that create falsehoods.

2. **It invokes perceptual changes** that can create adversarial situations where none existed.

3. **It limits relationships** by selecting and defining them.

4. **It invites illness** and shortens life.

The reason for this mental, emotional, physical, and relational toll is that Fear triggers our fight-flight response, which throws us into a defensive-aggressive posture. Our adrenal glands pump adrenaline and cortisol into the bloodstream, which sets our nervous system abuzz, tenses our muscles for hair-trigger response, and increases our rate of breathing.

Yet it doesn't end there. When we hold onto Fear, we end up living in a long-term state of nervous agitation, which can cause jumpiness, emotional volatility, and digestive issues.

Fear and Truthspeaking

Our ability to speak our Truth and hear the Truth of others can become short-circuited in insidious ways when we fall under the spell of Fear. It's because we then function more from our egos than our Heart-of-Hearts. Instead of trustingly and spontaneously sharing our feelings, we reduce risk by getting others to speak theirs first. One common way is to speak first and dangle a "How are *you* feeling?" out over our self-protective wall.

What's more, Fear does not allow us to be fully present and listen to Truth being spoken. Then when it comes our turn, Fear tempts us to color our Truth, in order to make it more palatable and less ego-threatening. We may also withhold some of our Truth, or try to replace it with illusion.

To help keep Fear from suppressing someone else's Truths:

1. **Tell** someone who asks you to speak your Truth before hers that you have learned that it is respectful to listen before speaking.

2. **Reassure** the person who is nervous or carefully choosing her words that her Truth is important to you, and that you are there to listen, not judge.

3. **Ask** the person struggling to speak at all whether he'd like to take a breath and speak a little later.

4. **Offer** to help her separate her feelings from her Truth, so that she can express each independently (which is easier and less threatening than together).

Breathe into Balance with Fear

Fear has a strong connection to breath. The Indian mystic Osho says that fast rates of breathing, such as when we are in intense emotional states, shorten our lives.[1] We hyperventilate, which—as illogical as it might sound—negatively affects oxygen delivery to the blood, muscles, and brain. This is known as *the Bohr effect*;[2] the reduced stamina and clouded thinking it entails compromise our Truthspeaking ability.

The converse is true as well: we can reduce the debilitating effects of strong emotions such as Fear—and increase stamina, blood oxygen levels, mental clarity, centeredness, and Truth-speaking ability—by reducing our rate of breathing. David McKenzie, head of Respiratory and Sleep Medicine at Sydney Australia's Prince of Wales Hospital, says we can tell we are breathing well when others do not notice that we are breathing. Taoist philosopher Chuang-tzu said the same thing 2400 years earlier, only a bit more poetically: *The breathing of the true person comes from his heels, while people generally breathe only from their throats.*[3]

As soon as you notice stress building, feel emotionally overwhelmed, or sense that your breathing is agitated and rapid, practice the following exercise. Please note that it is not a cure for chronic stress or anxiety, but rather a reprieve to give the clarity needed to embrace your Fear and have it guide you back to centeredness:

A Fear-Management Exercise

1. **Exhale slowly through your nose,** then relax with your lungs deflated for a count of about four seconds.

2. **Inhale slowly through your nose,** stopping at about half of your normal intake.

3. **Repeat Step 1.**

4. **Repeat the inhale-exhale sequence** ten times.

You should now feel more relaxed and clearheaded. If not, repeat the sequence another five times.

BREATHING AND SPEAKING

When we talk, we usually catch a quick breath through our mouths, so that we can keep on going. If we were to breathe through our noses, we would slow down and have a chance to collect our thoughts. It would encourage us to speak succinctly and use pause for effect, while also creating space for listening and for others to respond. When you find yourself rushing or stumbling over your thoughts, try breathing solely through your nose.

The Chapter at a Glance

Fear can tear at our Hearts and hijack our Truths if we ignore or overindulge it. When we welcome Fear as we would a respected guest to a Feast and feed him our presence and gratitude, we can hear what he has to teach us without being overpowered to the point of undermining our Truths.

Think of Fear as a Pony galloping across the prairie. Our lot is to ride the Pony, yet we have the choice of either being dragged under her belly or sitting up on her back. The prairie—our life—looks quite different when we are flopping around in the dust with sharp hooves pounding around us, rather than guiding the Pony with a full view the prairie and the wind blowing through our hair.

Fear comes to tell us his story. He may appear as a raging monster, yet he gets smaller and gentler the more we let him in. He can guide us to proceed cautiously, look at all angles, consider possible harm to self and others, prepare adequately, and think before acting. In these ways, Fear is our protector and loyal friend, always there when needed.

As one of our core emotions, Fear cannot be ignored or willed away. Trying to do so simply makes it reappear in another of its many shades: anxiety, panic, envy, aggression, jealousy, competitiveness, resignation, depression, feelings of inadequacy, or self-abuse.

In learning to embrace Fear, we broaden our perspectives, as *Fear is no more and no less than a lack of knowing.* When we hear noises in the night, we imagine them to be coming from the most threatening source. This Fear is not of the blackness, but of the unknown.

When we enter the unknown alongside our Fear, we can discern our limits without being held back by our perceived limitations. In exploring my Fear of heights, I found my limit by letting my Fear guide me as far as I could go, and I was content with that. My acrophobia is no more a limitation, as I am no longer paralyzed by what might happen if I were to push myself too far.

To embrace Fear, we must confront our fear of Fear. We need to leave behind the familiar and enter the unknown. When we go out into the night with a flashlight, we learn not about the dark, but about how to keep a distance from it by looking into it from the perspective of light. When we leave the flashlight behind, we develop eyes for the dark and discover the light that is already there. Now we can discover the dark's Truth.

Please note that this chapter's approaches to embracing Fear may not resolve fear-related anxiety or chronic stress. For that, seek professional guidance and the in-depth coverage in my book *Breaking the Trauma Code*.

Chapter Twelve Endnotes

1   Osho, *The Book of Secrets*, (St. Martin's Griffin, 1998), 50.
2   Christian Bohr, K. Hasselbalch, and August Krogh, "Concerning a Biologically Important Relationship – The Influence of the Carbon Dioxide Content of Blood on its Oxygen Binding," *Physiology Laboratory of the University of Copenhagen* (1904), http://www1.udel.edu/chem/white/C342/Bohr(1904).html#N_1_
3   Chuang Tzu, *The Complete Works of Chuang Tzu*, trans. Burton Watson (Columbia University Press, 1968), 78.

PART FOUR

FIXING WHAT SMOTHERS TRUTH

Every time I speak, I am in training for the next time I speak. The next seven chapters are devoted to engaging us deeper in the process of understanding and controlling the patterned emotional responses that can so easily conceal our Truth. We focus on seven Truth-masking expressions: gossip, small talk, swearing, absolutes, lies, humor, and secrets. They are all-too-common phenomena in daily discourse, and each one distorts our personal Truth—often to the point where it is unrecognizable.

Fortunately, the story does not end there. In the following pages, you will find clear and easy-to-follow ways to break the pattern of resorting to these Truth-squelching practices. Then I show you how to redirect your voice back toward Truth.

CHAPTER THIRTEEN

GOSSIP: A FAUX TRUTH

A piece of old-time farmers' advice states that if you like what I'm doing, tell others; and if you don't like what I'm doing, tell me. This addresses the fact that some people like to think of gossip as Truth's shadow, yet the Heart says that gossip is Truth's mutilator.

The less our ability to Truthspeak, the more our compulsion to gossip. I often see it as a yearning to Truthspeak, only disguised by hurt, jealousy, anger, or some other unexpressed feeling that is externalized rather than owned. For others, gossip is judgmentalism without courage.

At the same time, gossip has a seemingly positive side:

- **It serves as an emotional outlet** for those in expressively unfulfilling relationships. Gossip can provide a secret, intimate connection with somebody.

- **It empowers those who feel victimized**, by giving them a sense of having special knowledge about others. This can create a feeling of superiority, because the gossipers are privy to something that others don't know about.

Yet, the sense of connection and power that gossip provides is temporary and shallow. The sharing creates only an illusion of intimate involvement with someone, as it ultimately deflects Truth and dis-empowers.

"Gego dazhimaaken awiya (Don't say anything about anyone else)," I heard an Ojibwe Elder once say. She went on to explain that a person of Honor stands before the person of whom he speaks, rather than talking about that person behind her back. When she is not around, he only says something about her that he would speak in her presence.

The person of Honor goes directly to someone for information about him, rather than relying upon gossip or the opinions of others. In the words of another Elder, "Digging for facts is better than jumping to conclusions."

Why these uncharacteristically direct teachings from an Elder, when an Elder's normal way is by subtle guidance? The following legend shows why. Because of such teachings, the resounding and insidious effects of Gossip are common knowledge to most Natives. This legend, gifted to me by my mate, Woman-of-the-Four-Colors, illustrates these consequences.

The Woman and the Talking Feathers

South of here, on the banks of the great River that is born in the Mountains, stood a handsome Buffalo-robe lodge. It was nestled in a grove of Cottonwoods and had a tiny sweetwater Stream flowing beside it. Sun-Chaser and Snow-on-the-Leaves dwelled there, along with their first babe, whose name had not yet come.

It was on a day when Sun-Chaser was at the Riverside making a dugout canoe from a great Elder Cottonwood that the messenger from the Heron Clan arrived. In silence, they walked up to the lodge and sat around the outside hearth, the place of social gathering. The messenger was given the Place of Honor on the Sunset side of the hearth circle.

After food was served, as was the custom with visitors, the messenger spoke: "Snow-on-the-Leaves, I respectfully ask that you listen to these words: Your blood sister, Sits-High, is without mate. He, Cricket-Who-Runs, who was also my blood brother, journeyed out on the Prairie four Moons ago to scout the whereabouts of Buffalo. We have not seen him since. Not even our best hunters could follow his trail in the dry Grasses trampled by so many hooves. The only sign they found of him was his Pipe. We fear that he has gone on to another destiny."

In those days it was the tradition for a man to take in his mate's sisters and their children if they were in need and he was capable of doing so. Being young and talented, Sun-Chaser was already providing for several of the Elders and injured.

In honor of her mate, Snow-on-the-Leaves immediately turned to Sun-Chaser and said, "Beloved mate, your eyes have smiled kindly upon me and our child, and your hands are strong and giving. The Great Mother has provided well for us, and The Great Father has shined warmly upon us. I respectfully ask if you would take my sister, Sits-High, as you have taken me. I would be honored if you would shelter her and bathe her in the beauty of your Song."

In the waning of the Green Season, the two sisters and the man came together and became one lodge.

In the following White Season, Sits-High grew distraught. When she was around other People, she came to realize that she was not always first with Sun-Chaser, as she had been with Cricket-Who-Runs. She would feel her face grow hot when Snow-on-the-Leaves was referred to as Sun-Chaser's mate, or when Sun-Chaser would smile at Snow-on-the-Leaves rather than her.

Now Sits-High tasted the bitterness also and wanted to get rid of it. She began to spread rumors about Snow-on-the-Leaves to Sun-Chaser, and she shared tidbits of their private life with other People up and down the River.

As the White Season lingered, Snow-on-the-Leaves became despondent. Her mate, for some reason unknown to her, was not as warm and trusting as usual. She noticed more and more that others would look at her strangely and not talk as kindly with her as they once did.

One day, when the Waters were high from the melting of the Snows, Sun-Chaser and the sisters decided to take some extra Fish to their kin downriver. It was a warm, bright afternoon— the buds of the Cottonwoods were exploding and the Fish were moving into the shallows to spawn. Sits-High, not being needed to paddle, chose to stay behind and enjoy the day. She offered to watch the child.

She and the child, who was now out of his cradleboard and learning to walk, were down by the River watching the returning Geese. Before she knew it, the babe slipped on a wet Rock, tumbled into the Water, and was being swished down the River!

Sits-High hesitated for an instant while a shameful thought crossed her mind. Coming to her senses, she rushed to grab the babe, but he was gone!

She stood there in the shallows, as stone-still as an old Cottonwood stump. The Water chilled her to the bone, yet she could do nothing but stare blankly out over the River. The only sign of life from her was the tears finding their way down her face.

When dark descended, she dragged herself up the bank and started a small Fire. After throwing her clothes into the fire and burning off her hair, she rubbed their ashes into her skin. Then she walked through the night to reach the lodge of revered Elder Fragrant-Turtle, who lived with a sister clan down River.

"My intolerance and ungratefulness have caused a great travesty," she said to the Elder. "I was too full of myself to realize that I am my Circle, and that my Circle is me."

In an emotion-drained, monotone voice, she went on to describe all that had happened since her mate, Cricket-Who-Runs, disappeared.

When she finished, they both sat for a long time in the quiet of reflection. Then Fragrant-Turtle said these words: "Tomorrow, go ask the River for a Duck. Pluck all the feathers and put them into a basket. Then take it to the top of the high Bluff out on the Prairie and empty it to the Wind. Let the Wind scatter the feathers over the Prairie, then go gather each one. Come back to me only after you have found every last one."

A full Moon passed, and then another. Finally, Sits-High appeared back at the lodge of Fragrant-Turtle. Her cheeks were sunken and her eyes were glazed over like those of a dead Fish. In her basket were some feathers, but not nearly all of them.

"Grandfather," she said, "I have searched without stop, even after my feet wore bare of skin and left tracks of blood. I could not find all the feathers, but I did find my wretched self. The Feathers of my gossip that I scattered in all Four Directions with the Wind of my intolerance have traveled further than I could ever see or imagine.

"Each feather that I could find told me what it had done. Most of them landed deep in the recesses of People's souls, where I could not retrieve them. Yet few of them stayed where they first rested; they got blown on the next foul Breeze into another soul to infect, and then another.

"Even if all the misery I caused could be retrieved, I could not have brought it back. The burden would have been heavier than ten women could bear.

"I stand here, plucked naked and gaunt. All that clothes me is my shame. Why could I not have spoken my Truth, and have it heal me, rather than spread vile gossip and have it poison so many?"

* * * * *

The Four Ways Gossip Poisons

When we gossip, we impose our subjectivity (beliefs, biases, misinformation, self-interest) on ourselves and others, in these ways:

- We present our observations and evaluations as Truth.
- It often goes unquestioned.
- There is no perspective from the subject of gossip, which infringes upon Truth.
- We dishonor ourselves by disregarding our Heartvoices in favor of gossip.

In these ways, gossip poisons relationships, with both self and others. Let's take a close look at the four forms this poison takes:

1. **We disrupt the Balance within our Heart-of-Hearts.** It thrives only on its own Truth—the guiding voice that

157

comes from the collective input of mind, feeling, senses, intuition, and ancient memories. Each time we gossip, we give away some of the vital energy that is needed to empower our Truth. This occurs because personal Truth has its own energy, and gossip does not. We need to give some of our Truth's energy to the gossip in order to get it to take flight.

2. **The subject of gossip is dishonored by being deprived of representation.** Yet, this person bears the burden that gossip levies. No matter how gossip is justified, it is seldom a true or honorable echo of another's Truth. At the same time, the gossiper dishonors himself by presuming he knows her Truth and can involve himself in her life without her consent. *In the Old Way of Honor and Respect, one makes every effort to stand in front of someone when speaking about her. If it is not possible that she be present, we must be impeccable in both our speech and our motives for speaking about her. Otherwise, we will be haunted by the inevitable mistrust we create.*

3. **Gossip engenders more gossip.** Once it begins, it legitimizes itself and encourages more of the same. Over time, this taking of secondhand information for Truth corrodes the integrity of the circle of people involved. This leads to personal and relational imbalance.

4. **Gossip burns the gossiper.** There are no confidants in gossip circles—those who talk with you about others are just as willing to talk with others about you. Before you know it, lies are being hatched to cover backsides, and suspicion and mistrust inevitably creep into your relationships. Traditional Hawaiians have two sayings about this: 'Ai no ka 'īlio I kona lua'i[1]– A dog eats his own vomit; and He akua 'ai kahu ka lawena 'ōlelo[2]– Gossip is a god that destroys its keeper.

How to Identify Gossip

Politicians in the pre-mass communication age needed input from the public in order to determine what they considered important. According to a folktale, the politicians would send assistants to local taverns and inns, to "go sip some ale" and listen to the concerns people were discussing. "You go sip here, and you go sip there," the politician would say to his aides." Over time, *go sip* morphed into *gossip*. Yet it was not pejorative, as it referred only to local opinion.

With the passing of face-to-face communication, *go sip* took on a new form: some people found it tempting—and convenient—to assume what others were thinking and feeling. Over time, this detached way to *go sipping* became common practice. Now, many of us find it difficult to distinguish between Truth and gossip. When I am not centered, the line between gossip and Truth muddies as well. At such times, I use the following test to find the line. *If something fails any point of this test, it is likely gossip.*

It is Truthspeaking if:	It is gossip if:
The person being talked about is present.	The person is absent.
It has already been discussed with the person.	It has not been discussed.
The conversation is necessary.	The conversation is unnecessary.
It is a statement of circumstance.	It is a value judgment or hearsay.
It is helpful.	It is hurtful or derogatory.

As hurtful and out-of-Balance as I have found gossip to be, I still honor it as a teacher, because it:

1. **Reveals how much I still have to learn about the sacredness of speech.** Rather than castigate myself for gossiping,

I strive to honor the experience by recognizing it as an opportunity to improve my ability to communicate.

2. **Leads me to recognize contrary thought and speech patterns** that entice me to gossip. The better able I am to identify them, the more likely I am to address them.

3. **Warns me that I am not expressing a core emotion.** When I listen to the real voice of gossip, I can hear that the things I am projecting onto another are usually not about him, but about me. I find that what preoccupies me most about others is more often than not what I need to look at within myself.

Gossip certainly involves superficial communication about another; although when we sit with it, we might find that it is also an invitation for self-reflection. When we externalize our feelings through gossip, we cheat ourselves by missing the opportunity to better know and experience ourselves. At the same time, we prevent ourselves from more deeply knowing the person we are talking about.

GOSSIP AND MEDIA

Much of what we read, watch, and hear is gossip. Memoirs, biographies, and fiction expose the intimate details people's lives, even though we have no direct relationship with them. Very little of this literature is crass gossip, yet the written word (and media in general) perpetuate a culture in which we find Truth and relationship secondhand rather than one-on-one.

Does this mean we should quit media? I know a number of people (myself included) who have become very selective with reading and audio-video materials. I encourage those I counsel to be careful about reading simply for the sake of reading or turning to other media to have relationship needs met. Those options give us little opportunity to speak our Truth in the Now, and they seldom challenge us to heal.

On the other hand, when media serves our Truth, it transcends gossip and can help us to do the same.

A Cure for Gossip

We typically turn to gossip because of emotional woundedness or neediness. This points to the most potent cure for gossip: emotional healing. We might be able to quit gossiping through sheer willpower, yet we have not addressed why we turned to gossip in the first place. We are still wounded and unfulfilled, which inevitably drives us to yet another out-of-Balance way to try to get our needs met.

One big fringe benefit from addressing the underlying cause of our gossiping is that it can also help with other psycho-emotional imbalances, and thus enrich our lives in general.

Standing in our Truth is more empowering than gossip feigns to be. At a recent Truthspeaking workshop, a woman stated that a major consideration for whether or not she Truthspeaks is whether she thinks someone will gossip about what she shares. This is a common fear, which is based upon someone else's behaviors or values. In essence, we are putting more faith in the gossiper than in our integrity as Truthspeakers. This disempowers us—*we are basing our decision on who they are rather than who we are.*

By not Truthspeaking, we often end up creating demand for the gossip we are trying to avoid. Others want to know what we think and feel. On the other hand, there is little motivation for gossiping about a person who is clear, open, and present with his thoughts and feelings.

As you become more aware of the presence of gossip in your speech and that of others, try using this simple refrain (which I learned while attending Catholic elementary school):

> Small minds talk about people.
> Average minds talk about things.
> Healthy minds talk about ideas and values.

The Chapter at a Glance

Here we deepen the process of transforming our communication style by addressing the first of the seven common Truth squelchers: gossip.

Some claim that gossip is Truth's shadow; whereas the Heart says that gossip is Truth's mutilator. I have found that people engage in gossip because it seems to empower them and provide intimate connection through secret knowledge. Yet this is merely an illusion, as gossip deflects Truth, which disempowers and ultimately creates distance.

I once heard an Ojibwe Elder say, "Gego dazhimaaken awiya (Don't say anything about anyone else)." She went on to explain that a person of Honor directly addresses someone, rather than talking about that person behind her back. When she cannot be present, he only states what he would also say in her presence.

The person of Honor goes to someone directly for information, rather than getting it from gossip or others' opinions. In the words of another Elder, "Digging for facts is better than jumping to conclusions." Native Elders are uncharacteristically direct when it comes to gossip, as they know its insidious and resounding effects.

Gossip poisons all involved in these ways:

- It imposes the thoughts and feelings of others onto the subjects of gossip, while also denying them the opportunity to speak their own Truths.

- It disrupts the Balance within the gossiper's Heart-of-Hearts, by depriving energy and attention from the Truth.

- It gets mistaken for Truth, which engenders more gossip as people struggle to make sense of the resultant misrepresentation and mistrust.

- It burns the gossiper, as those who talk with us about others are just as likely to talk with others about us.

As hurtful and out-of-Balance as I have found gossip to be, I still honor it as a teacher. Gossip reveals what I can yet learn about Truth and the sacredness of communication. Thanks to gossip, I have come to better recognize and manage the triggers that entice me to gossip. And I have been able to start changing the thought and speech patterns associated with gossip.

Gossip can serve as a warning that we are not expressing a core emotion. When we listen to the real voice of our gossip, we will likely hear that what we project onto others is really about ourselves. What preoccupies us most about others is typically what we need to address within ourselves.

The best cure for gossip is to stand fully in your personal Truth. To determine whether you are Truthspeaking or gossiping, ask yourself the following questions: Is the person present who is being talked about? Has the topic already been discussed with that person? Is this discussion necessary? Is it relevant to current circumstances? Is it helpful? If the answer to any of these questions is "no," you are likely gossiping.

Chapter Thirteen Endnotes

1   Mary Kawena Pukui, *'Ōlelo No'eau, Hawaiian Proverbs and Poetical Sayings*, 11.

2   Ibid, 62.

CHAPTER FOURTEEN

SMALL TALK: WATERED-DOWN TRUTH

As valuable a contribution as language makes to clear communication, it can also get in the way. Whether we call it chitchat, the gift of gab, chewing the fat, or diarrhea of the mouth, the more we talk, the less we are heard. This entangles us in a boggling catch-22, as the less we feel heard, the more we tend to talk. In our work here, we'll simply refer to all run-on verbiage as *small talk*.

Oglala Lakota Elder Ote Kte (Plenty Kill) said that with his people, "the constant talker was considered rude and thoughtless."[1] When someone rambles on, we tend to distance ourselves from that person, either physically or emotionally. This can precipitate another unfortunate catch-22: the more one talks to create connection, the more isolated and lonely one feels.

The crux of these catch-22s is that the richness of words lies in their meaning. Yet the more words one uses, the less meaningful they become. Imagine someone's Truth as a spoonful of luscious soup that you are savoring. Though what if you first stretched that spoonful by mixing it into in a cup of water?

With small talk, listeners can feel dishonored when we expect them to sit through our verbal drivel. They drift off while we cloud our Truth to the point where its radiance barely shines through. Even if our audience doesn't desert us, there is a good chance we will suffer the aftershock: feeling alone, with our Truth going unheard.

Small talk cannot be Truthspeaking, because it is simply not the voice of the Heart-of-Hearts. Whether or not we do so consciously, we connect with our Heart-of-Hearts before

Truthspeaking. We then typically choose our words carefully, so that they best express our Truth. Any verbiage beyond that creates a countercurrent to clarity that can make it seem as though it would have been better had we not spoken at all.

How to Identify Small Talk

As we have previously discussed, words are the last step in communication. This gives us the opportunity to stop small talk before a word is spoken. Here is a simple test to screen what we are about to say.

It is Truthspeaking if:	It is Small Talk if:
I have chosen the topic to help express my Truth	The topic matter relates to something other than my Truth.
I have thought about what I'm going to say.	I am rambling.
It is necessary or relevant.	I am merely filling space.
I am speaking from my Heart-of-Hearts.	I don't know where my voice is rooted.
I am speaking clearly and to the point.	I am beating around the bush.
My audience has an interest.	I am going on regardless of interest.
I am not altering my Truth to fit the audience.	I am speaking primarily to please my audience.

This list can be boiled down to a single tip for recognizing chitchat: *ask yourself if you have lost the intrinsic connection with what you are sharing.* When you speak from your Heart-of-Hearts, you tend to feel invigorated, centered; when you drone on, you can feel flat and uninspired. Oftentimes small talk is fueled by reactive feelings such as envy and anger—another sign of disconnection.

Why Do We Small Talk?

As with healing in general, the better we know our imbalance, the more fully we can engage in our return to wellness. Small talk is symptomatic of a wounded ego, much like gossip and the other Truth-concealing patterns we will review in the next several chapters.

From what I've observed, the ego drenches us in a cascade of verbiage because we are experiencing:

- Discomfort with silence,
- A desire to entertain,
- Fear of sharing our Truth, or
- Fear of hearing another's Truth.

These reasons remind me of Oglala Lakota Elder Four Guns' reflection: "I have attended dinners among white people. Their ways are not our ways. We eat in silence, quietly smoke a pipe, and depart. Thus is our host honored. This is not the way of the white man. After his food has been eaten, one is expected to say foolish things. Then the host feels honored."[2]

When resorting to wads of words to find relief from anxiety, we directly and blatantly dishonor the Now. We are trashing it by filling it with fluff and trifles.

You might better understand small talk by revisiting the discussion of the human mind from Chapter 7. There, you read that what we typically refer to as the human mind is actually two distinct minds:

1. **The limbic system (or *intuitive mind*).** Here is the seat of our subconscious, long-term memory, pain, pleasure, motivation, and intuition.

2. **The neocortex (or *rational mind*),** which gives us the capacity for analytical thought, language, and spatial orientation.

Humans, you'll remember, are unique for having what may be the highest rational-to-intuitive-mind ratio of all mammals.

Our ego likes to have the rational mind do its bidding, and to deploy the word-based language associated with it. The more we turn to our ego, the more we resort to superfluous words for attempting to escape anxiety and find comfort. The ego can convince us that words are our salvation, even though we know in our Heart-of-Hearts that Truth transcends words.

What to Do When You Catch Yourself

Unlike gossip, small talk is not directly and blatantly hurtful (unless you are pained by boredom!). It is more like a chronic case of verbal diarrhea: draining, yet not life-threatening. The following exercise can help you get a grip on your rambling and redirect yourself back to Truthspeaking.

When you catch yourself small-talking:	How the exercise helps:
Breathe consciously, listening to your lungs filling. Exhale slowly, feeling the flow of the warm, moist Air.	Gives time to center and reconnect with your Heart-of-Hearts. Helps you feel comfortable with silence.
Remind yourself that words are the last step in communication, rather than the first.	Encourages the other voices of the Heart-of-Hearts to come forth.
Stay as close to the Raw Truth as possible.	Gives little opening or encouragement for small talk.
Choose rich, descriptive words, and only as many as necessary.	Keeps word-bites appetizing, and the listener attentive and hungering for more.

Here are three straightforward—and very effective—ways to keep from becoming a talkoholic:

1. Let others speak first.
2. Be careful not to interrupt others or complete their thoughts for them.

3. Practice the Truthspeaking basics of empathetic listening and concise speaking.

Yet no matter how diligently you manage your tendency to engage in small-talk, there will undoubtedly be times when it sneaks by you. Still, you can catch yourself by looking to your audience for clues. Are they ...

- Staring blankly, or are their eyes wandering?
- Talking amongst themselves or preoccupied with hand-held devices?
- Nervously shuffling or looking at their watches?
- Nodding and grimacing at the same time?

These clues are typically so obvious that you may begin feeling uneasy or self-conscious before you realize the cause.

"HOW DO I THEN TELL WHEN IT'S MY TIME TO SPEAK?"

Just as there are visual cues that point to small talking, you can watch for signs that indicate when it is appropriate to switch from listener to speaker. This occurs when a person...

- *Extends her hand in invitation,*
- *Steps or leans back and looks in your direction, or*
- *Ends her last sentence on a lower note or softens her voice.*

What Small Talk Can Teach Us

In the natural realm, everything exists for a reason. One of the gifts of small talk is that it helps us know our Longing (which, along with Fear, is one of our two core emotions). Becoming attuned to this emotion makes us more deeply aware of our need for relationship, whether it be with others or the world around us.

If we did not engage in chatter, our state of isolation might remain suppressed or disguised. When we can get in touch with the source of our small talking, it—like gossip— transforms itself into a beautiful healing gift:

- I can then choose to recognize my talking on not as a personal failure, but as an opportunity for improving my communication skills.

- When I know what tempts me to speak idly, I can better steer clear of it and redirect myself toward my deeper Truth.

With the awareness you now hold, you have the choice to take impediments to Truthspeaking, such as small talk and gossip, as either gifts or curses. The difference may seem to be only a matter of perspective, yet it is profound—it can create the opening you need to bring you solidly back to clearly expressing your Truth.

The Chapter at a Glance

The more words we use, the less meaningful they become. And the lonelier we become, as people tend to distance themselves from us. They do so because we have clouded our Truth to the point where it barely shines through. Oglala Lakota Elder Ote Kte (Plenty Kill) stated that among his people, "the constant talker was considered rude and thoughtless."[3]

Small talk doesn't qualify as Truthspeaking because it does not voice the Heart-of-Hearts. Whether done consciously or not, the Truthspeaker connects with his Heart-of-Hearts before speaking. He chooses his words carefully, so that they best express his Truth. Any additional verbiage is not only unnecessary, but it detracts from his Truth. Even worse, it can make it seem as though it were better if he had not spoken at all.

It is easiest to stop small talk before you have spoken a word. You can recognize it by asking yourself whether you feel connected with what you are sharing or about to share. Speaking from your Heart-of-Hearts is invigorating and centering, where small talk often leaves you feeling detached and uninspired.

Why, then, do we even engage in small talk? From what I've observed, it's either because we are uncomfortable with silence, we are trying to entertain, we fear sharing our Truth, or we want to avoid hearing another's Truth. It all boils down to dishonoring the Now with avoidance, fluff, and drivel.

Small talk is a product of our rational mind doing the ego's bidding. Both favor word-based language. Truth, however, is best expressed by utilizing a range of communication modes. Unfortunately, we lean heavily on words when we call up our ego at times such as when we are afraid to speak our Truth.

When you catch yourself chatting on, you can reconnect with your Truth by taking a moment to breathe and re-center in your Heart-of-Hearts. While doing so, remind yourself that words are the last step in communication, rather than the first. As you reengage in conversation, choose rich, descriptive terms, and only as few as needed.

If you want to check whether or not you are dragging on, glance at your audience. When they are staring blankly, focusing elsewhere, shuffling, or becoming preoccupied with something else, chances are you have drifted away from your Truth.

Like gossip, small talk is a barrier to Truthspeaking. When those of us who regularly resort to chitchat make the choice to change, our habit becomes our teacher. It tells us that one of the core emotions: Fear or longing, is going unexpressed. Knowing this can empower us to own our behavior, learn from it, and send it on its way.

Chapter Fourteen Endnotes

1 *Native American Wisdom*, ed. Kent Nerburn and Louise Mengel-koch, 24.

2 Ibid, 70.

3 Ibid, 24.

SWEARING: TRUTH GASPING FOR AIR

W ords best help us share our Truth when they are few and well chosen. In this chapter we explore how a certain class of words, variously known as cursing, obscenities, slurs, blasphemy, profanity, vulgarity, foul language, and swearing, can muddle our Truth and prevent it from being received with an open Heart. I use the term *swearing* as a catchall term for these forms of expression that in Civilized culture are generally considered to be offensive, disrespectful, or obscene.

Some people have become so articulate with swearing that they are able to be rude and indecent with great color and distinction. Unfortunately, as lucid as these nuances might be, they typically distract from one's personal Truth. When traditional Hawaiians hear swearing, they might say, Manene ka pepeiao—*The ears have an unpleasant sensation.*[1] Aggravated ears cannot discern Truth, and Truth needs to be heard in order to be honored.

A Closer Look at Swearing

A distinguishing feature of curse words is that they have both a literal and emotional meaning. The dictionary definition of a swear word gives its substance; however, its texture, power, and offensiveness are conveyed only through the feeling evoked by the word's usage.[2] In fact, swear words are primarily used for their emphatic emotional power, rather than for what they literally convey.[3]

Some people consider swearing to be a preferable alternative to physical violence.[4] While there is clearly a distinction between the two, cussing nonetheless often conveys abrasive—and even violent—energy. In this sense, swearing is more about the attitude behind the words than the words themselves. I can demeaningly spit out "You!" and it will in effect be cussing, even though the word itself is neutral.[5]

In our culture, the average speaker uses between 80 and 90 swear words per day.[6] This strong presence of obscenities has led some linguists to view them as the manifestation of an unconscious need to release strong emotional energy.[7] We choose swear words because they are more potent than civil language.[8, 9, 10] Calling someone a bastard is much more forceful and emotionally pregnant than stating that he is aggressive.

Even considering the plus side of swearing, there is no intrinsic need for it. Truthspeaking can be an equally effective and fulfilling way of expressing self, without the violence. Our pure Heartvoice is devoid of swearing overtones anyway; so to fully honor our Truth, we must express it in its pristine form.

Swearing and Our Culture

I find that many people are surprised to learn that, as with most hunter-gatherers around the world, the traditional Ojibwe people in the Lake Superior region where I live have no swear words. The closest they get is calling somebody a dog. Dakota Elder and historian Eli Taylor said, "In the Dakota language, no matter how long they sit and speak, no place, there is no bad swearing language, there is no using Tak Wakan's [the Great Mystery] name in swearing, nothing."[11]

Here are more voices echoing the same: a Benin Native is quoted as saying this in 1789: "We were totally unacquainted with swearing, and all those terms of abuse and reproach which find their way so readily and copiously into the languages of more civilized people. The only expressions of that kind I remember were 'May you rot, or may you swell, or may a beast take you.'"[12] Ohiyesa, the Santee Dakota we heard from earlier in the book, stated that "We found it shocking and almost incredible that among this race that claims to be superior there were many who...stooped so low as to insult their God with profane and sacrilegious speech!"[13] Zitkala-Sa, a Yankton Sioux, had this to say: "We send our little Indian boys and girls to school, and when they come back talking English, they come back swearing. There is no swear word in the Indian languages, and I haven't yet learned to swear."[14]

Why, then, do so many of us rely heavily on swearing? (64% of us use *fuck*, the litmus test for swearing.) Here are the most common reasons I've observed:

1. **Impatience.** We have come to expect immediate gratification and responses. When that is not possible, we get frustrated and angry.

2. **Acknowledgment.** Anxious to assert our point of view, we swear to either be heard above commotion or emphasize our point.

3. **Laziness.** Most curse words are nonspecific enough to apply to just about anything, and they're easy to grab when we don't have the right word at hand.

4. **Imitation.** We may be perpetuating a family pattern, wanting to fit in with others, or wishing to feel less secure.

5. **Rebellion.** Cussing is a quick and visible way to resist the pressure to conform. Adolescents, who are prone to stretching limits, have easy access to swearing-laced music.

6. **Release.** Many view swearing as a harmless expression of pain or a vent for overwhelming feelings.

In a nutshell, swearing is a palpable and common-enough practice in our culture that it can manifest in nearly any situation, for just about any—or no—reason. And it is becoming more accepted and practiced[15] which indicates that it is fulfilling a growing need for expression.

One major catch with cussing is that it ends up being only a temporary fix. While it can facilitate the release of energy from reactive feelings,

- It inhibits the expression of core emotions (see Chapter 10).

- The excess verbosity detracts from our Truth, and the tone smothers it.

- It does not capture the depth of our Truth, whether it be used as an interjection, insult, or space filler.

- It somehow gives license to make exceptions to respectful expression.

A RESPONSE TO SWEARING

We generally swear less around someone we admire. Yet what do we do when that person swears—especially if he or she is a close friend, relative, or mentor who leads an otherwise exemplary life and has much to offer?

Rather than come right out and ask "Why do you swear?" I practice the Truthspeaking principle of first listening. I observe how swearing fits into the person's life. Then I say something like, "I notice that you curse when you get frustrated; does it help?" Some enlightening conversations have followed, and several times the person has questioned her swearing habit and decided to address it.

The Truth Behind Swearing

Even though it is not Truthspeaking, it reflexively reveals truths about the person who does it. Here are some examples:

Swearing Phrase	Underlying Truth
"That fucking door won't open!" Lashing-out statements like "Go to hell," "That sucks," "God damn it!"	**Externalizing** You avoid personal responsibility for what you have experienced.
"What the hell did you do that for?" "Jesus Christ, what's the matter with you?!"	**Blaming** You focus on finding fault in others rather than empathizing.

Swearing Phrase	Underlying Truth
"What a pig!" Only a retard would do something like that!"	**Stereotyping** You label or pigeonhole others rather than seeing them as individuals.
"They lost the game; what buttheads!" "You whore—you're not married!"	**Judging** You assume the authority to evaluate others.
"What an idiot (jackass, dickhead, etc.)!" "He doesn't know his ass from a hole in the ground!"	**Belittling** You objectify or dehumanize others to assert power over them.

Two vibrant examples of the Truth behind swearing come from Andrew Huff, one of this book's editors. As a social worker on staff at a homeless shelter, he told me about this scene he recently witnessed: "Around 6pm, the door opened and a beloved guest, Hugh, appeared. We had not seen him in several months, so it was a thrill to see him. He came in and just about every other phrase he said was "Hey motherfucker!" or "How you doin' motherfucker?" But, in all honesty, there was such warmth in the room and the other guests were genuinely overjoyed to see him. It was an amazing opportunity to *feel* his language instead of hearing his words. In fact, there was a newer guest who hadn't met Hugh before and felt somewhat alarmed by the cursing. He asked me about it, and I said, "Actually, Hugh is one of the most caring, sensitive, kind men I know. He sounds like he's cursing, but he's really such a loving man.

"This reminds me of another guest who would frequently leave our office and say, 'God bless'—but it was *so* clear that what he meant was 'Fuck you.'

"When I recall both these examples I find myself noticing how the words really don't matter. Everything I needed to know was communicated without words. Like you've said many times,

Tamarack, words are at best symbols and distractions (when we use too many)."[16]

The bottom line is that we each want to be heard. Swearing is one way of doing so—if we don't mind *how* we are being heard or what swearing might be saying about us. Those who don't swear are often given more respect and listened to more closely than those who do; and they are typically considered to be more intelligent, self-aware, and emotionally mature.

A Truth-in-Swearing Exercise

Old habits die hard, which is particularly true with swearing, because we often resort to it in the heat of the moment. This gives us no time to consider options. The following exercise is designed to give us non-swearing alternatives that we can have on the tip of the tongue when we need them.

Make yourself a chart like the one below, and on the left side jot down the swearing phrases you commonly use. To the right of each, record the non-swearing alternative. Keep the chart handy, so that you can quickly refer to it when you need it. You might want to make copies and post them around your house, office, workshop, or car. Carry one in your pack, purse, or wallet.

Swearing Phrase	Alternative phrase
"God damn it!" "That pisses me off!"	"I'm angry!" "I feel overwhelmed."
"What the hell did you do that for?" "What a stupid idiot!"	"I don't understand why you just did that!" or simply, "Why did you do that?"
"Jesus Christ!" or "Oh, fuck!" particularly when you hurt yourself.	"Ouch!" or "Aaaahh!" They're oldies-but-goodies, yet they still work.
"What a pig!" "You lazy bastard!"	"What a mess!" "Will you help me with this?"

Swearing Phrase	Alternative phrase
"Go to hell."	"I won't do it."
"Fuck you!"	"I don't agree with you."

Here we see how thoughtless and inaccurate swearing can be. Changing old knee-jerk reactive patterns so that we can express what we see and feel without adornment takes speaking consciously and in the Now. This occurs spontaneously when we stay centered in our Heart-of-Hearts (see Chapter 6).

How to Change

With cussing having become so culturally ingrained, the only realistic way I know of to begin speaking with greater integrity is to approach it on a personal level. Here is the process I present in my Truthspeaking workshops:

1. **Know yourself.** The more you learn about yourself, the easier you can learn other things. When my son realized that he was visually oriented, he focused on geometry rather than algebra, which cured his frustration over math. Similarly, you can become more precise and intentional in the language you use to express your Truth.

2. **Say what you mean.** "That fucking car!" and "God damn you" mean nothing in and of themselves. Choose language that really says what you want to say. When you struggle for the right word or phrase, pause and take a breath. Remember that with Truthspeaking, you allow the Truth to emerge at its own pace.

3. **Work on your personal Healing.** The less old woundedness and pained memory you carry, the easier it is to not only accept, but cherish, yourself and others. Like so many others, you are then bound to realize that *swearing is not cherishing*.

4. **Observe others who swear,** imagining that it is you speaking. You may learn something about yourself and how you sound to others.

5. **Cultivate patience.** As with gossip and small talk, there will be times when you revert to swearing. Rather than chastising yourself, honor those moments for the lessons they teach. Use them to gauge your progress, and as an opportunity to commit more fully to change.

The Chapter at a Glance

Words best help us share our Truth when they are few and well chosen. However, swearing (my term for what is variously known as cursing, vulgarity, and the like) muddles our Truth and prevents it from being openly received. When a traditional Hawaiian hears such language, he might say, Manene ka pepeiao[17]– *The ears have an unpleasant sensation.* Unless we can clearly hear Truth, we cannot fully honor it.

Even though swear words may seem to be a good alternative to physical violence and aggression, swearing nonetheless transmits violent energy. This is conveyed not by the word itself, but by the feeling—or lack thereof—behind it. When I frown and forcefully say "You!" I convey so much more than the word, which is of itself neutral.

Swearing is common in our culture: the average person cusses between 80 and 90 times per day.[18] Still, as Truthspeakers, let us remember that there are less violent and more fulfilling ways to express ourselves. When we listen to the voice of our Heart-of-Hearts, we find that it is devoid of cuss words. To honor our Truth, we must learn to share it in its pristine form.

Many people are surprised when I tell them that the Ojibwe Natives in the Lake Superior region where I live have no swear words. The closest they get is calling somebody a dog. The same is true of the Dakota, who live out on the Great Plains west of us. Dakota Elder Eli Taylor said, "No matter how long [we] sit and speak...there is no bad swearing language."[19]

I have found that people swear for the following reasons: impatience, frustration, anger, laziness, imitation, rebelliousness, to assert ourselves, and as an emotional release. Unfortunately, venting via swearing ends up being only a temporary fix, as it does little or nothing to express the core underlying emotion.

Similar to the way verbosity masks our Truth, swearing can smother it in excess emotional energy. Yet if one pays close enough attention, she can still intuit some Truth. Someone using a cuss word will often be externalizing, blaming, stereotyping, judging, or belittling.

Even though swearing has become ingrained in our culture, we can change it in our lives by taking personal responsibility for it. The more self-aware we become, the more intentional we tend to be with the language we use to express our Truth. When the right word or phrase is not at the tip of our tongues, it's good to pause and take a breath. We need to be patient with ourselves. As with gossip and small talk, there will be times when we revert to using swear words. Rather than chastising ourselves, let's honor those moments as reminders of where we can improve—and of how much we have already improved.

Chapter Fifteen Endnotes

1   Mary Kawena Pukui, *'Ōlelo No'eau, Hawaiian Proverbs and Poetical Sayings*, 233.

2   Ruth Wajnryb, *Expletive Deleted: A Good Look at Bad Language* (Simon and Schuster, 2005), 69.

3   Timothy Jay, "The Utility and Ubiquity of Taboo Words." *Perspectives on Psychological Science* 4, no. 2 (2009): 155.

4   Ibid.

5   Luvell Anderson and Ernie Lepore, "What Did You Call Me? Slurs As Prohibited Words," *Analytic Philosophy* 54, no. 3 (2013): 352.

6   Timothy Jay, "The Utility and Ubiquity of Taboo Words," *Perspectives on Psychological Science* 4, no. 2 (2009): 156.

7   Ruth Wajnryb, *Expletive Deleted: A Good Look At Bad Language* (Simon and Schuster, 2005), 125.

8   E. Kensinger and S. Corkin, "Memory Enhancement for Emotional Words: Are Emotional Words More Vividly Remembered than Neutral Words?" *Memory & Cognition* 31 (2003): 1169–1180.

9   K. LaBar and E. Phelps, "Arousal-Mediated Memory Consolidation: Role of the Medial Temporal Lobe in Humans," *Psychological Science* 9 (1998): 490–493.

10 Timothy Jay, "The Utility and Ubiquity of Taboo Words," *Perspectives on Psychological Science* 4, no. 2 (2009): 155.

11 Dakota Eli Taylor, *Remember This!: Dakota Decolonization and the Eli Taylor Narratives* (Lincoln: University of Nebraska Press, 2005), 121.

12 Olaudah Equiano, *The Interesting Narrative of the Life of Olaudah Equiano, Or Gustavus Vassa, The African* (Self Published, 1789), 21.

13 Charles Alexander Eastman, *The Soul of an Indian and Other Writings from Ohiyesa*, ed. Kent Nerburn (New World Library, 1993), 8.

14 *Native American Wisdom*, ed. Kent Nerburn and Louise Mengelkoch, 21.

15 The Associated Press Profanity Study, Ipsos Public Affairs, March 23, 2006.

16 From a March 31, 2019 conversation with the author.

17 Mary Kawena Pukui, *'Ōlelo No'eau, Hawaiian Proverbs and Poetical Sayings*, 233.

18 Tony McEnergy, *Swearing in English: Bad Language, Purity and Power from 1586 to the Present* (Routledge, 2006), 31.

19 Dakota Eli Taylor, *Remember This!: Dakota Decolonization and the Eli Taylor Narratives*, 121.

CHAPTER SIXTEEN

ABSOLUTES: NEVER SAY NEVER

In Chapter 2, we discussed the nature of Truth as being personal and ever-changing, rather than singular and absolute. This awareness has long been held by many traditional people. The Sandawe, a band of southern Africa's San people (who many anthropologists consider to be representative of the original human culture),[1] have a saying: *I am bringing food to the house for you* ([cl] mancha-s /lwaka koo-na-s hapu-me-s ?ie),[2] which implies that each person's Truth brings nourishment to the band.

You may also remember from Chapter 3 that recent linguistics research shows use of the pronoun "I" to be associated with honesty, while absolute statements tend to lack the pronoun. As we are about to explore, the language of absolutes leads us away from Truthspeaking and toward the manipulative speech discussed in Chapter 4. Unequivocally stated observations, beliefs, and convictions reinforce the notion of a singular and unchanging Truth. These are among the most controlling and repressive forms of speech, as they leave no room for doubt, ambiguity, or questioning.

Is There Absolute Truth? Absolutely Not.

The philosopher Voltaire said that murder is murder—unless it's done in large number to the sound of trumpets.[3] Depending on the era or the victor, a person could either be put to death or honored as a hero for the same murder. *Where is the truth in that?* One person loves me for who I am and the next person hates me for the same reason. *Where is the truth in that?* This holy text says I am destined for a life of eternal bliss, while the next holy text virtually assures me eternal damnation. *Where is the truth in that?*

I believe the problem lies in the fact that we often act as Truth*seekers* rather than Truth*speakers*. The difference may be subtle—but it is key—as the former turns our attention outward, while the latter asks us to look inward. As Truthseekers, we feel compelled to search for Truth in others, while as Truthspeakers we listen for our own Heartvoice. There is no need to *seek* Truth when we already have it within us.

Yet one of our cultural myths is that Truth is to be found "out there" somewhere. The Ojibwe Elders I studied with believed otherwise: that Truth dwells in the Heart of each individual, and it is that person's Truth alone. Each person's Truth is held as sacred, the Elders stated, and nothing is to be said or done about it unless it impinges upon the Truth of another. Even then, a way is sought to allow both Truths to coexist.

If we were to see ourselves as organs within an organism, the liver's Truth might be quite different from the lungs'. Yet both are equally important for the health of each organ, as well as for the health of the organism. If one organ's Truth were placed above the other—or if one tried to live the Truth of the other—the entire organism would suffer.

In our conformity-based culture, an individual's Truth can appear to conflict with what authorities claim to be The One Truth. Without adherence to it, these authorities fear their power would be usurped; so to encourage compliance, they often create fear by claiming that society would collapse without adherence to their Truth.

Many of us have so bought into the One Truth myth that we wonder how our hunter-gatherer ancestors survived all those hundreds of thousands of years without The One Truth. This leads to the notion of Native people being ignorant savages leading miserable lives—and that their enlightenment will come when they are ready to forgo the right to determine their own personal Truths.

A Closer Look at Absolutes

Who hasn't heard or said "You're absolutely right" or "I'm with you 100 percent" many, many times? Does this mean that someone else is absolutely wrong, or that I am against someone else 100 percent? To a listener, it could be taken that way. And sometimes it is.

Like us, our words cast a shadow. *Whatever we say that does not come straight from the Heart and acknowledge a greater reality conveys a silent, unstated message that can speak louder than our words.* Another way of looking at it is that every action has its equal and opposite reaction. It is a law of language as well as physics.

Yet only in our fabricated binary reality are there just two forces or choices. Add the power of belief to our question-answer, this-that, and right-wrong scenarios and they become absolute.

Only it doesn't end there, as absolutes perpetuate and entrench dualistic existence.

We can defuse this trap and return to living our Truths by simply substituting absolute-defining terms with ones that allow flexibility and give options. To jumpstart the process, I have created a table showing some of the most commonly used absolute terms and openness-creating alternatives for them.

Absolute Term	Alternative
All/Every	Many, most, several, nearly all
Always	Commonly, repeatedly, very often
Certainly	Possibly, conceivably
Impossible	Unlikely, improbable, implausible
Is	May be, could be
None	Few, not many, scarce
Never	Uncommonly, rarely, hardly

How Labeling Limits

We often unintentionally make absolute statements by labeling. In and of itself, labeling facilitates communication by using a single term to describe or identify something that would otherwise take lengthy explanation. It is easier to say that someone is a plumber than to describe what he does.

At the same time, labels have their drawbacks:

- **They can stereotype,** which either disguises or denies a person's individuality.

- **They are often used judgmentally,** whether or not judgment is consciously intended.

- **They can be imprecise** or confusing.

Here is an example of the latter:

A young child asks, "Mommy, why are those two girls holding hands and kissing?"

"Because they are lesbians."

The child gives his mother a confused look, which causes her to realize what she did—and didn't—do. She adds, "Because they love each other."

The child then understands, and she smiles.

My criteria for using labels are that they help me to best express myself, and that they don't hurt anyone. This is in keeping with the Zen aphorism found in the Part I introduction: Speak your Truth without punishing.

JUDGMENT AND TRUTH

Criticism and Judgments lead to beliefs, upon which we base our opinions. It looks like this:

Judgment —> Belief —> Opinion

Here we can see that our opinions are three steps removed from our Truth. When instead we start by expressing our Truth about something, we tend to be more accepting and less judging. We are then less likely to formulate a belief, then an opinion, based upon a judgment. Instead, we tend to be more self-accepting and open to the Truths of others.

Negatives Stifle

In our culture, absolutes often take the form of negatives. When we use terms such as *no, don't, won't,* or *can't,* we create distance between ourselves and others. *Never,* the most extreme negative, is also the costliest, for these reasons:

- It leaves no options.
- It denies reality, as in reality there are no absolutes.
- It tends to alienate and hurt others.

It is important to address not just the *use* of negatives, but also the *tone* of speech, as in this example:

A woman asks her partner, "Would you like to make love tonight?"

Reply option #1: "No; I'm really tired, I need to get some sleep."

Reply option #2: "I'd like that. Only I'm beat: it's been a rough day, so I don't know that I could be very present. Yet after a good night's sleep, it could be different!"

Which answer would you prefer to receive? In essence, they both say the same thing, yet they each convey a different message. Where #1's tone conveys self-absorption and could trigger feelings of rejection, #2's tone is sensitive and accommodating. The difference lies in the fact that the second reply contextualizes the "no" as temporary, rather than absolute.

Giving consideration to tone and context helps us to constructively express ourselves, along with building rapport. "I never want to see your brother again," could look like this: "My sinuses repeatedly feel terribly irritated when I'm in your brother's smoke-filled apartment. How about if we invite him over here more often, and we can ask him to smoke outside?"

WHAT A BUT DOES

People commonly use but to soften a negative statement, as in "I like your friends, but I don't want to hang out with them anymore." At the same time, we have set up good/bad or yes/no comparison, as well as diminishing whatever precedes the but. Rather than honoring both Truths, we have them competing with each other. This often results in confusion, and it can trigger strong emotional responses. We can avoid these pitfalls by clearly and directly expressing our thoughts and feelings (more in Chapter 4).

A Negatives Awareness-Raising Exercise

Get a visceral feel for the debilitating effect of negatives and the uplifting power of positive speech by practicing this exercise with someone emotionally close to you. This exercise can also be effective in clinical and professional settings.

1. **Express something negatively,** as in the previous "Would you like to make love" example.
2. **Give a moment** for the feeling to sink in.
3. **Express the same thing positively,** as in the previous example.
4. **Give a moment** for the feeling to sink in.
5. **Ask your partner how the first statement felt** in comparison with the second.
6. **Switch roles** with your partner, so that you can consciously experience both sides of a negative-positive statement, and so that you can both grow from the experience.

The Exercise for One

If you don't have a partner, construct a box similar to the one below, record in the left-hand column the negatively-phrased statements that you recall using and in the right-hand column, rewrite your remarks as though you were Truthspeaking.

Following is an example of how to practice this exercise. I left the last few statements un-revised, to give you an opportunity to begin practicing.

What I Usually Say—Negative Statement	What I Could Say—My Truth
"I like him a lot; I just don't want to be with him tonight."	"I'm confused about my feelings for him."
"Thanks for sharing your beliefs, but I wish you could have stated them more briefly."	"I want to understand you better. It would help me if you could be more concise."
"No, I'm too stressed to go to a movie."	"I like that movie. Will you take me another time when I'm not so stressed?"
"I never have any time for myself."	"I'm feeling overwhelmed and need some solitude."
"Yes, I have money, but I have bills to pay."	"I feel uncomfortable when you ask me for money; I'd like you to earn your own."
"I can't believe you said that."	"I'm surprised and hurt by what you just said."
"Why don't you ever listen to me?"	
"I think I gave the best performance, but I didn't finish first."	
"I don't want to do the dishes."	

WHAT IT TAKES TO CHANGE

With consistent repetition, you can reprogram yourself to speak your Truth, rather than resorting to negatives. Here is how to do it:

- *Practice one of the above exercises at least twice a day. Fifteen minutes after your practice, review what you covered, in order to imprint it in your long-term memory.*

- *Ask those you work and live with you to flag you when you state something negatively. Immediately transform it to a direct expression of your Truth.*

The Chapter at a Glance

In Chapter 2, we discussed how Truth is personal and ever-changing. People in traditional cultures have long understood that Truth is plural, not singular or absolute.

As we explored in this chapter, the language of absolutes leads us away from Truthspeaking and toward manipulative speech patterns based on unquestioned observations, beliefs, and convictions (as covered in Chapter 4). They reinforce the notion of a singular and unchanging Truth. Here we find the height of manipulative language, which removes all semblance of doubt or questioning from personal Truth.

Too often we act as *Truthseekers* rather than *Truthspeakers*. The difference is subtle, but key, as we turn to others with the former, while with the latter we look inward for our own Heart-voice. There is no need to *seek* the Truth when we already have it within us.

Yet one of our cultural myths purports that Truth is out there somewhere for us to find. With the Native people I've come to know, Truth dwells in the Heart of each individual, and it is his or her Truth alone. Each person's Truth is held as sacred, and nothing is to be said or done about it—unless it impinges upon the Truth of another. And even then it does, a way is usually found that allows both Truths to exist.

We of the civilized era are accustomed to Truth being established from above, which leads to conformity. This prompts some of us to wonder how our hunter-gatherer ancestors survived for thousands upon thousands of years *before* the advent of institutions to generate Absolute Truth.

Our culture's notion of Absolute Truth casts Indigenous people as ignorant savages leading miserable lives and waiting to be enlightened—which is predicated on sacrificing the right to determine our personal Truth.

We are all familiar with the phrases like "You're absolutely right" and "I'm with you 100 percent." Like other absolutes, they have a shadow side: they imply that someone else is absolutely wrong, and that I am 100 percent against someone. *Everything we say that does not come straight from the Heart and acknowledge the greater reality carries a silent, unstated message, which sometimes speaks louder than our words.*

You can honor your Truth, and the Truths of others, by avoiding absolute terms and providing context to what you say. When you say "No," are you sure that's the message you want to convey? When responding to your intimate partner's request to make love, there is a world of difference between replying with "No," or with "Yes; I'm also really tired right now. I don't think I could be present with you the way I'd like to be. How about if we get a good night's sleep, then make love in the morning?" By giving context and clarity, the second response speaks the deeper Truth of the "No."

Chapter Sixteen Endnotes

1 Victoria Gill, "Africa's Genetic Secrets Unlocked," *BBC*, last modified 1 May 2009, accessed 22 April 2019, http://news.bbc.co.uk/2/hi/science/nature/8027269.stm.

2 Gerard M. Dalgish, "Subject Identification Strategies and Free Word Order: The Case of Sandawe," *Studies in African Linguistics* 10, no. 3 (1979): 273-310.

3 Voltaire, "Rights," in *Questions sur l'Encyclopédie* (1771).

CHAPTER SEVENTEEN

LIES: TRUTH BURIED BY FEAR

I f we are innately Truthspeakers, why do we have the capacity to lie? Is it a paradox, or might there be another explanation? In this chapter, we deconstruct the truth-lie dichotomy, then learn to read the Truth within the lie. At that point, the two merge as shades of the same awareness.

Yet the journey to the point where the concept of lies ceases to exist as a counterpoint to the concept of Truth can be a rocky one. For many people, the myth of lies turns out to be the most challenging aspect of Truthspeaking to embrace, as it rocks the very foundation of our culture.

Finding Relationship

Although we tend to think of *truth* and *lie* as diametrically opposed, we intrinsically know that the two are intertwined. Telling a lie depends on first knowing the truth—we can only make the decision to lie *after* we know what the truth is.[1] Creating an effective lie depends on the truth: the closer the two are, the more likely the lie will go undetected.[2, 3, 4]

Despite the close relationship of the two, we find it hardest to hear another person's Truth when we suspect that it is a lie. Virtually all of us have grown up being told that to tell the Truth is good, to tell a lie is bad—even a sin—and that a lie could never be the Truth. Perhaps we were shamed or punished for lying, because it was willful deception. Whatever the case, we're taught that a lie is the direct opposite of Truth.

The Native Elders I apprenticed with showed me another way with lies, so that I could learn to embrace them as Truth.

A liar then became a Truthspeaker to me, expressing her Truth of the Moment. The concept of the lie became just another myth—another example of our culture's dichotomous approach to life.

"No way!" is the reaction I get from more than a few people at Truthspeaking workshops. "What about fork-tongued politicians and used-car salesmen? And how about conniving rapists and those who sweet-talk the elderly out of their money?"

For the Truthspeaker, not only are all lies Truth, but all Truths are lies. In the next section, we begin exploring how Truth is embedded in a lie, but first let's take a look at how all Truths are lies. Each person's Truth is—and can only be—a subjective interpretation, reflecting sensory input, beliefs, and history. One version of the well-known tale of the blind men and the elephant has each man describing the elephant based upon what he touches. One claims the elephant to be like a tree (leg), another says she is like a fan (ear), and a third states that she resembles a waterspout (trunk). They end up arguing amongst themselves and calling each other liars even though each is speaking his Truth of the Moment.

Recognizing that all Truths are lies, I am slow to discount what a person I perceive to be a liar says. Yet my lies are no different than anyone else's lies. If I believe theirs because of the deeper Truth they hold, why not mine as well? Lies not only reflect, but help create, our realities. That being the case, my lie reflects what I would like my reality to be. By lying, I am then helping to manifest my lie; i.e., I am making it Truth.

Now, let me show you how "lies" speak Truth, with an event recounted from two different perspectives.

"I Didn't Do It"

Imagine that you suspect a neighborhood child broke your garage window. When you question her about it, she responds, "I didn't do it."

If you are a typical person, the first thing you will do is judge whether or not she is lying. Children have amazing perceptive abilities—they can usually tell when they are being judged. The child then feels threatened by someone unrelated and more powerful than her.

That makes her reality very different from yours. If she did break the window, you want to know whether or not it was an accident. That is not important to her. Instead, she is thinking, "I'm afraid I did something wrong and won't be accepted for it— I'm going to be judged and punished." That is *her* Truth.

In order to help keep you focused on her Truth, I will not tell you if she actually broke the window. Or if we knew she did break the window, I would not tell you whether it was accidental or intentional. Those "facts" are not important, as they have nothing to do with her expression of Truth of the Moment.

When you cling to those facts, you act like a Truth*seeker*— your violated ego seeks external answers to assign blame disguised as responsibility. You divert yourself from matters of the Heart. The ego, having no feel for the Heart-Truth, doesn't realize that it cannot be found in facts or accountability.

The result of your ego's efforts is that the child has been stymied from directly expressing herself, which is the *opposite* of what you had originally wanted. By asking for facts, she became intimidated, as she knew intuitively that she was going to be judged rather than heard.

Finding Truth in a Lie

What would it look like to hear the Truth in what you presume is the child's lie?

Instead of hearing her say "I didn't do it," you would hear, "I'm afraid."

Yet the way of our culture is to focus on the facts—the window is broken and your property is damaged—and treat as a lie any perception that does not hold those facts sacred. That is why you think someone is not speaking Truth when it doesn't fit what you have predetermined to be "right". Those who do not speak the Truth—*your* Truth—are then liars.

The trouble is that as soon as you label someone a liar, you have shut yourself off from the Truth they are trying to express.

If you were to remember that Truth is in the Now, you could still honor the reality of the broken window along with the child's feelings in that moment. Her Truth is about both, which were crying out to you in that I-didn't-do-it "lie."

Perhaps you are now able to see that those four words of hers: "I didn't do it," were actually a complex expression of her Truth. The bottom line is that labeling her statement a "lie" is an unfair oversimplification of what was going on.

HOW TO LISTEN TO A LIE

Once we are aware that Truth is nested within a lie, we are responsible for relearning how to listen to the person behind the words. Here is an abbreviated three-step method to help clear the way for the Truth in lies. This process reawakens our innate ability to listen without judgment.

1. **Become aware of your reactive feelings** *(see Chapter 8) and cultural conditioning. You cannot control your patterned responses until you can identify them.*
2. **Recognize their effects upon you.** *While suppression and denial make them stronger, recognizing the role they play breaks their subversive grip and brings them into the light, so that they may be healed and released.*
3. **Center in your Heart-of-Hearts.** *Truth cannot be heard without an open Heart to receive it. Being in a nonreactive, nonjudgmental state allows you recognize the Truth behind the "lie." To review how to do this, see Chapter Four.*

The Tough Ones

The previous example illustrates how and why virtually all lie-labeling occurs. However, not all "lies" will be as easy to interpret as that one—especially when they are paired with cleverness, power, and complex feelings.

When the CEO of a logging company puts a positive spin on unregulated deforestation, it might be very hard to hear him crying out for acceptance because his father never acknowledged his abilities. We see only the magnitude of his lie, rather than the magnitude of the hurt that led him to create it.

The Truth of a loved one who says she never wants to see you again may be even harder to hear. How, through the emotional trauma you yourself feel, can you be expected to hear her saying that she is simply too hurt and out-of-control to trust in her love for you?

In our culture, lies are chimerical and pervasive. Still, there is only one response to them all: listen for the Truth behind them. I'll be the first to acknowledge that it's often easier said than done. When someone is rubbing my face in deceptive language or doublespeak, I can struggle to maintain perspective and listen with my Heart. What helps me is remembering that:

1. **The Truth that a lie speaks is not denied by my inability to hear it.** That is why, no matter what I *think* I hear, and no matter from whom, I serve the Truth by extending Honor and Respect.

2. **One Heart naturally knows the voice of another Heart.** By listening non-reactively and nonjudgmentally, I will be better able to discern the Heartvoice of another. When I quiet my ego, I can more easily hear through the din of another's ego.

The truth of any matter can be found within the Heartvoice. One of my Elders told me that we cannot lie when we speak from our Heart-of-Hearts.

"Why is that?" I asked.

As is customary, he did not give me a direct answer. Through the guidance of his well-phrased questions, he helped me realize that because our Heart-of-Hearts is the wellspring of our personal Truth, lies could not possibly originate there. The sensory, mental, feeling, intuitive, and ancestral voices that join to form the Heart-of-Hearts are each already their own Truth. Like begets like, so how could their collective voice—the Heart-voice—be anything but Truth?

The Heartvoice is our center, our seat of Balance. It resonates our essence and speaks our pure Awareness-of-the-Moment. How could that ever be right or wrong, Truth or lie? For the same reason that we do not speak lies when we speak from our Heart-of-Hearts, we do not hear lies when we listen from our Heart-of-Hearts.

What Creates the Illusion of Lies?

A lie is the ego refusing to let the Heartvoice be heard. A lie is the product of a moral or religious code that asserts the right to judge and label. When someone has said something that isn't sanctioned by the code, he has lied. Among humans, a lie is an expression of fear—it is the fear that fills a child, or the child within anyone, when she doesn't feel safe enough to speak her Truth.

When someone else tries to adopt my Truth, it becomes a lie. My Truth is personal: it begins and ends with me. That being the case, my Truth becomes a lie to everyone else. If I try to convince someone else to take on my Truth, I am attempting to either deceive him or rob him of his own Truth. If I were successful, my Truth would become his belief system, not his Truth. This, by the way, is how religions are born.

Words do not convey Truth—they tell a story. The good storyteller can perhaps dance close to the Truth, and the deceiving storyteller can dance around the Truth. He might even be able to create the illusion of Truth. To embrace a story as Truth is to create a lie.

When we listen from the Heart-of-Hearts, we find that words are only one of many expressions of its voice. Intent, feeling, and intuition are all part of how the Heart speaks. We thus hear the Truth of a story not in its literal words, but in what they draw forth. Here is why the second listener in the example a few pages back could hear the child's Truth; and why the first person, who listened only to her words, heard a lie.

Discerning Heart from Ego

Listening with intent, feeling and intuition is how we hear the Heartvoice through a wounded ego's attempt to create a faux Truth. Think of it as listening with a *third ear.* We can help our third ear listen by remembering that the Heartvoice:

- **Tends to be soft and complex,** while the ego's voice is typically straightforward and lacks depth.

- **Asks for openness and discernment** in order to be heard, where the ego's voice needs only another listening ego.

- **Travels slowly from one Heart to another,** with little fanfare. The ego's rushed voice can project with the hullabaloo of a preacher on a crusade.

This is not to discount the ego's voice. When it serves our Heartvoice, it contributes to our Truth. It's only when the ego— or any other part of our Heart-of-Hearts—overrides our Heartvoice that we lose centeredness and risk becoming numbed to all but the most raucous of voices.

A key component in discerning the Heartvoice from the ego is the ability to attune to instinctual responses and gut reactions. As deceptive and smothering as the words of a dominating ego can be, we still typically have gut reactions to them. This innate discomfort is a signal from our Heart-of-Hearts to not accept the words for face value, and instead to listen to the Truth that emerges between them.

To our detriment, we often ignore our gut reactions. If we were able to embrace them, they could help us distinguish clear Heartvoices from the warped pleas for love and understanding that we often call lies.

The following exercise is designed to help recognize pleas from the ego for what they are. The kinds of ego statements found in the first column need to be spotted because they are typically the prelude to "lies." These statements are preliminary distortions of Truth that often become amplified and lead to lies when they do not produce the desired results.

TRUTH-EXTRACTION EXERCISE

What I hear (her ego)	My gut reaction (my Heartvoice)	What she is really saying (her Heartvoice)
"I feel your pain."	"That's unlikely."	"I have suffered too much alone; I'm looking for empathy."
"You need this item."	"How would *you* know that?"	"I'm looking for validation of my self-worth. The only way I know to get it is to have People buy something from me."
"I have found the One True Political System/ Faith; come join me!"	"I feel coerced; I feel that I'm not being respected for the individual I am."	"I don't know myself, and I fear my own mortality. The more People I can get to join me, the more secure I feel."
"I don't trust you."	"I feel distanced and belittled."	"I don't trust myself enough to open up to you and accept who you really are."
"I didn't do anything wrong!"	"I am not accusing you."	"I don't trust in my own Heartvoice; I'm looking for validation from others."
"I'm mad at you." or "I'm depressed from being with you."	"I'm feeling blamed."	"My self-esteem is low and I feel vulnerable, out of control, so I'm taking care of myself by pushing you away and blaming you."

What I hear (her ego)	My gut reaction (my Heartvoice)	What she is really saying (her Heartvoice)
"I didn't get much sleep last night." or "I lost out again."	"I can't feel sorry for you."	"I need to play victim, because I don't know how to offer myself empathy and I need it from others."

Repeat the exercise until you gain an intrinsic feel for the different voices. Then you can bring the exercise home by personalizing it in this way:

1. **List five ego statements** *similar to those in the first column that you have used in the past week.*
2. **Dig beneath the words** *to find what your Heartvoice is trying to communicate.*
3. **Now list five ego statements** *you have heard others use over the past week.*
4. **What were your gut reactions** *to those statements?*
5. **What do you intuit** *their Heartvoices as saying?*

The more you practice this exercise, the better you will get at hearing others' Truths, even though they may be ego-distorted.

How We Script Someone Else's Truth

When we respond to a lie—or any other statement—from the ego rather than the Heart, we fall into the trap of looking for the Truth we want to hear, which is known as *Fishing*. In doing so, we deny our Heartvoice and discourage others from speaking theirs. We get locked into a self-serving communication pattern that overrides our innate desire to hear another person's Truth—essentially for one Heartvoice to connect with another.

What determines whether or not a statement is Fishing is our intent. When we say or do something not primarily to communicate, but to get something, we cast our words out as bait, rather than to share Truth.

Fishing takes two forms:

1. **Reject someone's Truth and manipulate for a desired response** by asking "Why do you feel the way you do?" "Why do you always...?" "Why can't you ever...?" or similar. We are typically Fishing for an apology or admission of guilt.

2. **Bait to meet a need.** When we ask what someone thinks about something we said or did, we may be Fishing for an ego boost. Another form is giving a complement for the sake of receiving the same in return, such as with "I like what you're wearing."

In essence, then, Fishing is attempting to manipulate others' Heartvoices in order to comfort our egos. For that reason alone, Fishing—no matter what form it takes—cannot be construed as true and honest communication.

When I'm asked what can be done about Fishing, my first response is, "Don't take the bait." As tempting as it might be, rest assured that there is a hook buried in it. Often the easiest way to tell whether or not you're being baited is by the uncomfortable feeling you get when someone's trying to get you to nibble.

EFFECTIVE PATTERN BREAKING

As much as we like to think we are creatures of intellect and volition (after all, we are Homo sapiens: the thinking human), I estimate that up to 98% of our thoughts and actions are based on habit and pattern.[5] That means we need to consistently catch our patterned behaviors in order to change them. To do this effectively takes the help of those around us, as it is near-impossible for us to constantly catch our own behaviors when we do not execute them consciously.

Sometimes when we go Fishing, we do it unawares. Yet there are two common clues: feeling anxious or full of expectation. Both are indications that we need a certain response in order to feel satisfied. If we were truly asking open-ended questions, we would have no reason for expectation or anxiety.

When we are in trusting relationships and supportive of each other in our healing, we can agree to call each other on our Fishing and replace it with Truthspeaking. Fishing is a habitual behavior for almost everyone who practices it, which makes these two pattern-changing guidelines vitally important: catch it right away, and do it consistently.

Honoring the Liar

As incongruous as it might sound, liars warrant our empathy and attention. When we judge a person a liar or Fish for a desired response from her, we dismiss her personal Truth and cut off the hand that she had extended for help. The lie, though it affronts our ego, may have been the only way she was capable of reaching out. To hear the Truth beneath her lie requires that we first grant her honor and respect.

Pablo Picasso said that art is a lie that tells the truth.[6] The artist creates an illusion that helps form the viewer's Truth. If we do not allow the artist her brushstrokes, we will never see the picture she envisions. When we encourage the artist, perhaps we will be blessed with the picture of her Truth.

Following is the only guideline we need in order to encourage—and keep open to—the expressiveness that conveys Truth.

Accept

We have come to know that there is Truth to be heard in every moment and every voice, and that language is often inadequate to convey it. We have learned that a "liar" is often a person sensitive to judgment, and he likely suffers from fear of rejection. We now recognize that our role is to offer acceptance and support by listening intuitively and compassionately.

In the Circle Way, Giving opens the doorway to Receiving. When we can extend ourselves to the person who has lied, we might have the rare privilege of viewing his most beautiful Truth-painting. When we can look beyond the false dichotomy of truth *versus* lies to see truth *in* lies, it will seem as though the clouds have opened to let The Sun shine through. We will have renewed our intrinsic awareness that everything exists or occurs for a reason, and that everything we are given is a Gift to be cherished.

In contrast to that, we become victims when we think someone is lying to us. We might feel deceived and become mistrusting. We reason that if a person is lying—and he must be if we can't hear his Truth—he is either trying to get something or get away with something. We then become judgmental and believe we must hold him accountable. Here, *Giving is Receiving* works just as well: we have given judgment, and in exchange we have received tunnel vision, along with becoming deaf to the voice of Truth.

It is equally important that we accept ourselves. One Heart naturally knows the voice of another Heart. Yet when we lack faith in our own Heartvoice, we tend to become mistrustful of another's. Our ego then performs a dark feat of alchemy— she transforms Truth into a lie. The glistening gold of clarity degrades into the dreary lead of deception.

Truth in Lies Exercise

Here is practice in embracing lies, along with learning how to recognize when we don't. The training will help us in those moments when we are on the cusp of either seeking the Truth or seeing it as a lie.

How to Honor a "lie"	How to dishonor a "lie"
First honor my own Heartvoice.	Mistrust the "liar."
Listen from my Heart-of-Hearts.	Label and judge his story.
Be fully present.	Make assumptions.
Listen with complete acceptance.	Interject when he is speaking.

Forget about facts; open to intent, feeling, and intuition.	Assume that his Truth is only his words.
Listen to my gut reaction.	Be swayed by his title, reputation, or credentials.
Recognize that what is right differs from person to person.	Distance myself from him.
Admit that any block to another's Truth is actually my block to my own Truth.	Feel victimized by him.

In many African languages, the terms for *chameleon* and *liar* are the same. That doesn't necessarily mean, though, that lying is an evil act. Most plants and animals lie, and we humans are no exception: we have a history of lying that goes back to the dawn of our species. If we did not lie, we would have gone extinct long ago.

When we (or any other predator) utilize camouflage, we lie to our prey. When we bait a trap, we tell some hapless animal that he has an easy meal awaiting him. When a carnivorous plant passes her insect trap off as a nectar-rich flower, she lies as well.

At the same time, she is telling the Truth, by revealing and acting upon her need for nourishment. Often whether we judge a lie as right or wrong depends on which side of the trap we find ourselves.

I suggest that we embrace a more nuanced view of lying, in order to see the rhymes of Truth within. The two work together to create a more complete picture than either gives us alone. Here is a rhyme of my own to echo that awareness.

When we believe in lies
we draw between us lines
which are savagely dividing
and send all truth to hiding

Perhaps if we could listen
to lie's voice often hidden
we'd hear the pleading wail
of a child's Heart grown pale

What if with lies we'd dance
and start a new romance
With truth and lie as lovers
we'd find balance with all others

The Chapter at a Glance

It is a paradox of human existence that while we are innately Truthspeakers, we nonetheless have the capacity to lie—to mislead and allow the ego to reject the Heartvoice. We most strongly refuse to hear another person's Truth when we suspect that it is a lie. Virtually all of us have grown up being taught that to tell the Truth is good, to tell a lie is bad, and that a lie is the polar opposite of the Truth.

However, as growing Truthspeakers, we learn that there is no such thing as a lie. Everything has its own Truth—its own reason for being. In addition, Truth is personal: my Truth begins and ends with me. That makes my Truth a lie to everyone else. If I try to convince someone to adopt my Truth, I am attempting to rob him of his own Truth. If I were successful, my Truth would become his belief system, not his Truth.

For a Truthspeaker, there is one response to all lies: listen for the Truth behind them. We begin by connecting with our own Heartvoice. One Heart naturally knows the voice of another Heart; meaning that when we are centered in our Heart, we can best discern the Truth of another.

The sensory, mental, feeling, intuitive, and ancestral voices that join to form the Heart-of-Hearts are each already their own Truth. Like begets like, so how could their collective voice—the Heartvoice—be anything but Truth? For the same reason that we do not speak lies when we speak from our

Heart-of-Hearts, we do not hear lies when we listen from our Heart-of-Hearts.

To hear the Truth beneath the lie requires that we first extend honor and respect to the liar. If we judge a liar, we dismiss her personal Truth and cut off the hand that she had extended for help. The lie, though it pains our ego, may have been the only way she was capable of reaching out.

The only guideline we need in order to encourage—and keep open to—the Voice of Heart is *acceptance*. We have learned that there is Truth in every moment and every voice, and that it lies beyond the realm of language. We have come to know that instead of being a liar, the person is probably sensitive to judgment and suffers from fear of rejection. We realize that our task is to extend him Honor and Respect by listening intuitively and empathetically.

When we think someone is lying to us, we become victims. Often we feel deceived, and we see the person as either trying to get something or get away with something. We then become judgmental and want to hold him accountable.

One Heart naturally knows the voice of another Heart. Yet when we lack faith in our own Heartvoice, we find it hard to trust in another's. We are then prone to interpreting what we hear as lies.

Chapter Seventeen Endnotes

1   J.J. Walczyk et al., "Cognitive Mechanisms Underlying Lying to Questions: Response Time As a Cue to Deception," *Applied Cognitive Psychology* 17 (2003): 755–74, http://dx.doi.org/10.1002/acp.914.

2   Ibid.

3   I. Hershkowitz, "A Case Study of Child Sexual False Allegation," *Child Abuse and Neglect* 25 (2001): 1397–1411, http://dx.doi.org/10.1016/S0145- 2134(01)00274-5.

4   A. Vrij, P.A. Granhag, and S. Mann, "Good Liars," *The Journal of Psychiatry and Law* 38 (2010): 77–98.

5   S.J. Gershman et al., (2016) "Plans, Habits, and Theory of Mind," *PLoS ONE* 11, no. 9 (2016): e0162246, https://doi.org/10.1371/journal.pone.0162246.

6   Alfred H. Barr Jr., *Picasso: Fifty Years of His Art* (New York: Arno Press, 1980).

CHAPTER EIGHTEEN

HUMOR: SUGARCOATED TRUTH

We all benefit from humor, because we each have an innate sense of humor. It is literally a sense, in the same way that touch and smell are senses. Wit and laughter are universal and part of what defines us as human.[1]

In the same way that intuition embodies the philosopher Nietzsche's concept of the *third ear*—that which allows us to listen beyond words and grasp the Heartvoice—our sense of humor can be considered our *fourth ear*. Nietzsche considered laughter to be the Voice of Truth.[2] Humor serves as our watch-tower, our critic, our reminder to remain humble.

Humor is oblivious to power, status, and convention. With humor we can take on another persona, which allows us to step back from ourselves and be self-critical. This is necessary, because we cannot know the Forest with our face up against a Tree. Levity opens us to other perspectives—including the nonsensical, sarcastic, even offensive—because levity takes us beyond our norms and the rules we live by.

Yet therein lies a quandary: without the rules we live by, someone not solidly grounded in her Heart-of-Hearts can, with-out even knowing it, easily slip into a dishonoring use of humor. Because humor has the capacity to either cradle or disfigure Truth, we must approach it with deliberation, intention, and empathy—the same qualities that inform our Truthspeaking and Truthlistening.

At the same time, we must remember that humor is powerful precisely because it pushes boundaries *and* because it at times crosses them. As we do with our personal frontiers, we must risk going too far with mirth in order to find our niche with it.

This chapter will not teach you how to be humorous. Much like Truth, humor is personal and ever-changing. We each have a unique relationship with humor, and we each use it in ways that best serve us. This chapter is intended to help you better understand when Humor serves Truth and when it does not.

Truthspeaking as Laughter

Roger Jack, an American Indian from the Pacific Northwest, had this to say when reminiscing about his Aunt Greta: "She always said good Indians remember two things: their humor and their history—These are the elements that dictate our culture and our survival in this crazy world. If these are somehow destroyed or forgotten, we would be doomed to extinction. Our power gone."[3]

Laughter's power lies in its ability to prompt connection. It is a highly contagious social experience—we can be made to laugh by simply hearing another person laugh[4] and are 30 times more likely to laugh when we are with another person than if we are alone[5, 6]

Whether coming from a Native contrary (such as the Lakota Heyoka), medieval jester, or contemporary satirist, the seeds of humor are considered such Gifts that the humorist is honored in all cultures I'm familiar with or have studied. Let us also honor the humorist in us—the one who is always there to take us beyond the assumed limits of our sight. We can do this in two ways: seeing laughter as a healing force, and learning to laugh at ourselves.

Why We Honor Humor

With its ability to open healing channels, Humor has become a key component of Positive Psychology and holistic wellness.[7] Laughing invigorates the physical system, lowers blood pressure, and aids digestion. As great therapy for depression, laughing triggers the release of endorphins (which are natural antidepressants) in the brain. Even more, laughing soothes the emotions and helps release tension. Comic relief is stress relief.[8, 9]

Both Truth and Humor are personal. Just as we need to hear our own Truth before attempting to know another's, Humor cannot be extended to others honorably unless we first know how to laugh at ourselves. An Elder once suggested to me, *"Gidaa-baapi'idiz bishigochigeyan*—Laugh at yourself when you make a mistake."* She said that the ability to chuckle rather than grumble would help me remember that there are no mistakes: that everything happens for a reason.

Self-deprecating (self-critical, belittling) humor is a double-edged sword: In one sense it can help to keep us humble, and at the same time it can be an indicator of low self-esteem. Here's how to tell the difference: When our self-effacements are accompanied by feelings of rejection and victimization, they only help erode our sense of self; and when we can smile at our own foolishness and accept it as a teaching, chuckling at ourselves is centering.

Humor has allowed me to step back and gain perspective, rather than slapping myself with some stern self-judgment. When I would trip on an exposed root, my usual reaction would be to berate myself for being so unaware. That would entrench me all the more in my self-image of being a klutz, a slow-learner. When I started to respond with the likes of, "Hey root, you're quick! Let's see if you can pop up out of nowhere and catch me off-guard again," it changed my attitude and challenged me to grow.

When we can joke about ourselves, we keep our ego in check. When we kid around about rules and traditions, we keep them connected with real life, which keeps them fluid and changing. When we joke about our hardships, we open ourselves to their Blessings. Recently someone asked how I was doing with the cold I was nursing. I told her what a treat it was: that it made me feel as though I was on vacation. After I explained that the cold was a welcome break from the health crises I just pulled through, we both got a laugh out of it—and it helped me maintain perspective and Thankfulness.

Humor and Love

I've heard it said that Humor is as important in life as love. I have found humor to be so central and intrinsic to mated love that I regard it *as* love. Here's why:

1. Humor acknowledges the Beauty and uniqueness in another. With humor I can:
   - Give my mate a compliment *and* a smile.
   - Challenge her wit, which gives radiance to her intelligence and perspective.
   - Show her that she is worth the extra energy that an amusing exchange requires.

2. Humor is part of the Beauty and uniqueness of another. My mate uses humor to:
   - Give spice to an otherwise run-of-the-mill exchange.
   - Snap me out of a rut.
   - Help give me a new outlook.
   - Accentuate her allure.

3. Humor gives the perspective that keeps relationships vibrant and growing.

4. Humor opens the doorway to listening and acceptance.

5. Humor is balm for healing the wounds of relationship.

6. Without humor, relationships grow shallow and bland.

Recent research indicates that the happiest married couples are those with the greatest ability to use humor to help manage difficult conversations.[10] Just as important, let us not forget that humor can be just plain fun—another essential ingredient for a vibrant relationship.

The Pitfalls of Humor

While Humor can provide levity when needed, if misused it can knock the wind out of some people and make them feel disrespected. We need to remember that the perception of humor is a personal matter, which means that what I find hilarious might strike another person as deeply hurtful.

To laugh at ourselves and not others is to use humor respectfully. We can be the butt-end of our own jokes; however to extend that to others without their consent is dishonoring. It can so easily be taken as criticism or an insult. Being able to joke about ourselves is a matter of personal awareness—we each need to find our own sardonic twist in order for it to be effective.

At the same time, it can be both respectful and healthy to laugh at others—*when they are laughing with us*. When they see the humor in their actions, them being on the receiving end of a joke is neither demeaning nor alienating. Here it is important to know the people we are joking about/with, as it is usually those with whom we have close, trusting relationships, and who have a solid sense of self, who can roll with—and enjoy—self-directed jokes.

Sometimes people use Humor as an ego booster when they feel uncomfortable in social situations, or when they want to make an impression. They might want to sound clever, or they are out to demean somebody else in order to look better themselves. They could be attempting to create alliances. While these tactics may appear to be effective in the short run, they are bound to backfire, as they serve a False Truth and smother the voice of our Heart-of-Hearts.

What Makes Humor Cruel?

Jerry Lewis said that the premise of all comedy is a man in trouble.[11] The reason comedy allows us to laugh at our folly or misfortune is that it illustrates the predicament without the pain. When the pain is used for a laugh, it is no longer comedy but malice.

How can one tell when humor is being used out of Balance with the Heart? One nearly sure way is to tap into your sense of empathy. Imagine that *you* are on the receiving end of the humor, and see how it feels. If you are in fairly good emotional health, your Heartvoice will tell you whether or not the humor is healthy.

If you have some imbalanced behavioral or emotional patterns, they may mask or distort your Heartvoice. With low self-esteem, you may not perceive deprecating humor. When I'm unsure of my own perspective, I will ask an emotionally healthy person whom I trust to be my *deprecating Humor barometer*. I'll try out my humor on her to get her reaction, and I'll do the same when I am the recipient of questionable humor.

HUMOR IS SUSPECT WHEN IT IS USED TO:

1. *Soothe tension between People without resolving the source of the tension.*
2. *Say something serious in a light way. While it may make for easier delivery, it dilutes the message, which interferes with fully hearing it.*
3. *Mask feelings.*
4. *Camouflage criticism and judgmentalism.*
5. *Escape from reality. "Lighten up—life is for living!" and "Let's have some fun and not take things so seriously," are often-times cover-ups for lack of self-love and fear of Walking one's given Path.*
6. *Get a laugh at another person's expense. Besides not having the therapeutic benefits of healthy humor, victim humor can cause hurt and erode self-esteem.*
7. *Stereotype How can we presume to know the Truth of another person's identity when we can only know our own Truth?*

How to use Humor Healthily

A unique quality of beneficial humor is that it is like planting a seed: it nurtures growth in Awareness, and in doing so it repays the sower many times over. However, using out-of-Balance humor is like spreading the seed of an invasive alien Plant. Let us be very mindful of what kind of sowing we practice.

Healthy humor is a sign of Walking in Balance. Yet we have too few role models for nurturing humor, and most of us are emotionally wounded in one way or another, so we can benefit from some additional guidance. The following guidelines, though no substitute for a healthy culture and the clear voice of the Heart-of-Hearts, are offered so that they might be of help during the healing process. Use humor:

1. **As an icebreaker when approaching a touchy or overwhelming subject.** After the opening is made, it is important to then get serious and focused. Humor can also serve as a diversion to break out of a rut in an oppressively solemn situation.

2. **To diffuse collective stress and build camaraderie.** The natural tension that sometimes builds up during a focused group activity can be dispersed by humor. When we can laugh together, we can usually share in other ways.

3. **To share feelings.** The language of humor sometimes conveys feelings that are otherwise too elusive or sensitive to express.

4. **To express hard-to-grasp ideas.** Humor can deliver in a few words what would otherwise take a lengthy description.

5. **As an Awareness-raising tool.** It is used occasionally and selectively by Elders and Masters to help Seekers break through impediments to Awareness. Here is an example from the Zen tradition: *A Master once asked a new Seeker; "Where are you from?" The Seeker fidgeted for a moment, then said, "I am from an emptiness created by form." "Most interesting," replied the Master. "I am from*

the next province." Using Humor in such a way requires that the Seeker have a high degree of trust, attunement, and knowledge in order for the practice to be effective and not detrimental. Because of the tremendous risk for inappropriate usage, using humor in this way is nothing to be toyed with by someone who does not have the traditional background and training to do so.

6. **To regain centeredness.** When we slip into imbalanced behaviors, denial, or addictions, humor may be able to give us some space and time to get a grip. When we start seeing in black-and-white, humor can give us back our view of the Rainbow.

The old saying that *what humors us, makes us wise* has survived because of its intrinsic Wisdom. Humor can wake us up, stimulate us, and focus us on something we might otherwise miss.

Humor in all things...

... is my motto in Life. Even in the direst and most tearful circumstances, there is a pearl of mirth or a satirical edge. It is there for a reason—as a Gift to help keep us from getting too nearsighted, or from becoming self-righteous to the point of tyranny.

Our species evolved humor as an innate sense for two vital reasons: *if we can't laugh, we can't be serious*, and *if we can't laugh, we can't know our Truth*. Without the clear eyes and centeredness that humor helps us maintain, we are not able to keep perspective in approaching the important matters of life. The Gifts of a healthy, functioning sense of humor are essential for Balance in the Heart-of-Hearts. They are to Truthspeaking what rich Earth and sweet Rain are to a growing Flower.

In leaving this topic, it is important to grasp one fundamental concept: *our personal reality—the way we manifest our seriousness, our Truth—is no more than a personal envisionment*. In other words, *envisionment creates reality*. Humor allows for the fullness of envisionment, because it breaks through boundaries, frees the mind, and stimulates creative juices. Seeing the world with the help of a "third eye" allows us to embrace boundlessness and experience the Circle Way with wit and whimsy.

The Chapter at a Glance

We all have a sense of humor, which is literally a sense, in the same way as touch and smell. Similar to how intuition functions as our third ear, Humor acts as our third eye. It is our watchtower, our critic, our reminder to remain humble. It opens us to other perspectives—the nonsensical, the sarcastic, even the offensive—because much of what could benefit us dwells beyond convention and the rules we live by.

Like Truth, humor is personal. Every person draws the line between humor and slander differently. We must approach humor with the same qualities that inform our Truthspeaking and Truthlistening: deliberation, intention, and empathy. We can be pretty sure humor is out of Balance when it is used to mask feelings, camouflage criticism, escape from reality, stereotype others, or soothe tension between People without resolving the source of the tension.

On the other hand, healthy humor can be used to diffuse collective stress, build camaraderie, serve as an icebreaker when approaching a touchy or overwhelming subject, and raise our Awareness of something we might otherwise miss. Whether coming from a Native contrary (such as the Lakota Heyoka), medieval jester, or contemporary satirist, the seeds of humor are considered such Gifts that the humorist is honored in all the cultures I am familiar with or have studied. Let us also honor the humorist in us—the one who is always there to take us beyond the assumed limits of our vision.

We can begin to do this in two ways: by seeing laughter as a literal healing force, and by and learning to laugh at ourselves. An Elder once suggested to me, *"Gidaa–baapi'idiz bishigochigeyan*—Laugh at yourself when you make a mistake." She said that the ability to chuckle rather than grumble would help me remember that there are no mistakes; that everything happens for a reason. When we can smile at our own foolishness and accept it as a teaching, our self-deprecation is healthy.

To that end, my motto in Life is: *Humor in all things*. Even in the direst of circumstances, there is a pearl of mirth or a satirical edge. It's there in such situations for two fundamental reasons— to keep us from becoming nearsighted, and to protect us from the scourge of self-righteousness.

If we can't laugh, we can't be serious. Without the clear eyes and centeredness that humor helps us maintain, we are not able to keep perspective in approaching the important matters of life. And if we can't laugh, we can't know our Truth. The Gifts of a healthy, functioning sense of humor are essential for Balance in the Heart-of-Hearts. Humor is to Truthspeaking what rich Earth and sweet Rain are to a growing Flower.

Chapter Eighteen Endnotes

1 D.A. Sauter et al., "The Universality of Human Emotional Vocalizations," *PNAS* 107, no. 4 (2010): 2408–2412.

2 Jason M. Wirth, "Nietzsche's Joy," *Epoché: A Journal for the History of Philosophy* 10, no.1 (2005): 117-139.

3 Shirley Ann Jones, *Simply Living: The Spirit of the Indigenous People* (Canada: New World Library, 1999), 29.

4 R.R. Provine, "Laughing, Tickling, and the Evolution of Speech and Self," *Current Directions in Psychological Science* 13 (2004): 215–8.

5 Ibid.

6 R. R. Provine and K. Emmorey, "Laughter Among Deaf Signers," *Journal of Deaf Studies and Deaf Education* 11 (2006): 403–9.

7 Bruce D. Kirkcaldy, *The Art and Science of Health Care: Psychology and Human Factors for Practitioners* (Hogrefe Publishing, 2011), 277.

8 L. Bloch et al., "Emotion Regulation Predicts Marital Satisfaction: More than a Wives' Tale," *Emotion* 14 (2014): 130–44.

9 J.W. Yuan et al., "Physiological Down-Regulation and Positive Emotion in Marital Interaction," *Emotion* 10 (2010): 467–74.

10 Ibid.

11 Alan Dale, *Comedy is a Man in Trouble: Slapstick in American Movies* (University of Minnesota Press, 2000), front flap.

CHAPTER NINETEEN

SECRETS: THE LAST FRONTIER

All living Beings—except Civilized Humans—dwell fully in the Now. Because of that, they are naturally and spontaneously honest. Their secret? It is simply that they have no secrets. That is the essence of Truthspeaking.

Unlike the rest of creation, we cling to our past. We carry it around with us like so much dirty laundry that keeps accumulating, rather than living it out in the moment it arises. Much of this laundry takes the form of secrets, which fall into two categories:

1. **Secrets we keep from ourselves,** such as unexpressed guilt, shame, and feelings of inadequacy.
2. **Secrets we keep from others,** such as unshared feelings, unmet needs, resentments, and jealousy.

The Personality of Secrets

As with Truth, secrets are personal. Their content, how they are perceived, and the way they are handled is unique to each of us. Below you will find a range of perspectives on secrets from a discussion about secrets that individuals were keeping from the group to which they belonged. The setting was a national forest, where twenty-five adults and seventeen children, ranging in age from three to seventy-five, participated in a year-long wilderness immersion program. They lived in bark shelters and snow caves, foraged for much of their own food, and learned skills such as firemaking, primitive cooking, and tracking. As much as those types of skills were needed, my staff and I placed even more emphasis on the group process and conflict resolution skills that made healthy, long-term group living possible.

Students were to bring only the gear specified on their packing lists. They were preparing for a minimalist experience, with the focus on being inventive and getting by with less. No books or field guides were allowed, as storytelling was to provide the entertainment, and students were to learn directly from nature, the staff, and each other.

Of particular concern in the following conversation were items individuals brought that were not on the packing list. Note the range of perspectives on secrets that were expressed, and listen to the Truth each person reveals about his lifestyle and upbringing. In the same way we can intuit the Truth behind a Lie (see chapter 17), we can discern some of each speaker's Truth from how he treats a secret. Here is a transcription of the dialogue.

Person 1: "Hiding things is bringing ideas from the outside culture, and it may not be necessary here. I don't have anything not on the packing list"

Person 2: "I think there is absolutely nothing I wouldn't tell every person in this clan about what I've done here. I don't necessarily feel that I need to know everything about everybody, although I know for myself that the energy around holding a secret is not conducive to feeling open."

Person 3: "I wanted to bring some things out, and I left them behind at the last minute. And then I kicked myself for not bringing them. I have a history of holding secrets, and my whole life I have held secrets. When I was a child, if I really expressed what I wanted to do, it would not have been allowed. This is a really good topic for me to work with, and I'm glad we are bringing it up. I'd just like to encourage anyone who is keeping something to open up, so we can talk about it and find ways to get our needs met through each other and this place."

Person 4: "I have nothing. I stuck to the packing list and I don't think I have anything to hide."

Person 5: "It's not really a secret that I have a handful of items that were not on the packing list, but I don't need any of them. I don't even know why I brought them."

Person 6: "I brought a tennis ball to roll on and work out sore muscles. I was going to get rid of it by sneaking it out of here somehow. As far as secrets, I have an inner child who creates a lot of secrets and fantasies, and I really don't want to go through them all."

Person 7: "I'm not aware of any secrets. My inner realm is sometimes secret from others, but also secret from me."

Person 8: "I took the list very seriously. I think secrets are different for different people: what is a secret for one person might not be for another. In my life before this course, I sang every day at sunset, in thankfulness for the day. I always did it secretly, and now some people know."

Person 9: "I brought a book: *The I Ching*. I thought for a long time if I should bring it along. I want to explain why I brought this book to anyone who'd like to know. Please ask me."

Person 10: "I want to say that I feel really strongly that the trust we are building in this circle, along with the whole Truthspeaking model, is going to support this process of people becoming more communicative and honest and really looking at what their needs are. I feel like this issue will sort itself out."

Several people said they felt lighter after divulging their secrets, and nearly everyone said that the sharing brought the group closer together. All but one person chose to release the items they had that were not on the packing list.

How to Receive Secrets

Our relationship with secrets, much like that of lies, can be paradoxical. Some of us are of the opinion that secrets are of concern only to the secret-keepers. Yet by definition, secrets are interpersonal. They play a significant role in shaping the relationships of secret-keepers and those from whom secrets are kept. The same is true for those who share secrets.

When a person decides to share a secret with us, the Truthspeaking way is to receive it in the same way we would receive her Truth: with acceptance, support, and non-judgmental empathy. Along with this being the guidance I received from Elders, research has found this to be the most helpful way to create a safe environment for a secret to be shared and received[1, 2]

Yet it can be very hard to share a secret when it comes right down to it. Going back to Addie in chapter 3, she confronted her fears of uncleanliness and disconnection by sharing with her wilderness camp group that she had a sexually transmitted disease. Her process was made easier by the fact that her campmates extended their open Hearts.

Secrets in Relationships

Mated people live longer,[3] one reason likely being that they have someone with whom to share secrets that are important only to them. Confidences kept between a couple encourage trust and deepen intimacy, both of which strengthen their relationship.

HEART TALK

In a relationship, it is not the secrets themselves that create connection, but rather it is the level of intimacy that keeping secrets creates. The depth of this intimacy depends on the ability to be fully present and listen attentively. One way to cultivate it is to whisper. My mate Lety and I often whisper to each other in private, not because we have to, but because of how special it makes our sharing, and it encourages us to give each other our undivided attention. We call our practice Heart Talk.

There is a saying that *to know you is to love you*. To complete the circle of relationship, let us include the inverse as well: *to be known is to be loved.* When we live from the Heart, we tend to *want* to share our hidden pasts and veiled selves—those deep, dark, and seemingly contrary aspects of ourselves—with those closest to us. A Truthspeaker strives to hold no secrets. I consider being fully transparent with another to be the most fundamental definition of love.

If we are to be Truthspeakers right from the beginning of a new relationship, we might invite our new partner to talk with our previous partner(s). When we are serious about fostering no illusions, breaking old patterns, and establishing new ways of communicating, we have nothing to fear and everything to gain. No matter what past relationships entailed or how they ended, they were our mirrors, and they tell the precious story of who we are in the most pure and intimate way.

The Consequences of Secrets

Although we have the capacity to keep secrets, let us remember that it is not our heritage. The practice is only a self-protective adaptation to the economy of scarcity that replaced nature's abundance when we abandoned our hunter-gatherer ways for a controlled-resource economy.

A life based on maintaining secrets creates the need for endless cover-ups. Shame and self-destructive tendencies are the inevitable results. Even so, most people decide to keep secrets anyway, because they fear rejection or disapproval from those close to them[4, 5, 6, 7]

The unfortunate fallout is that when we expect this reaction from others, we preemptively distance ourselves from our Circle, which cuts us off from the very connections we so desire. It is the *act* of keeping secrets—not the secrets themselves—that leaves us feeling disconnected.

On the other hand, the reverse—disclosing secrets—typically leads to improved mental and physical health.[8] This occurs because when we let go of our secrets, we reduce our stress level and free up the psychic energy to more fully embrace life. Traditional Hawaiians have a beautiful saying for such an uplifting state of being: Hu'ea pau 'ia e ka wai,[9] which means *all scooped up by rushing water.*

This chapter concludes Part IV of our return to Truth. In the following chapters, we create an envisionment for the blossoming that can occur when we invite others to rediscover their Truths with us. The return to Truthspeaking might begin as a personal journey, yet its full power and beauty manifests only when it starts to ripple through our lives and relationships.

The Chapter at a Glance

All living Beings—except Civilized Humans—dwell in the Now, which makes them naturally and spontaneously honest. Their secret? It is simply that they have no secrets. Therein lies the essence of Truthspeaking.

Unlike the rest of creation, we cling to our past and haul it around with us like so much dirty laundry that keeps accumulating. Rather than taking care of it and walking on burden-free, we hold onto much of it as secrets. There are two kinds of secrets:

1. **Secrets we keep from ourselves,** such as unexpressed guilt, shame, and feelings of inadequacy.
2. **Secrets we keep from others,** such as unshared feelings, unmet needs, resentments, and jealousy.

Although we have the capacity to keep secrets, it is not our heritage, but rather an adaptation to the economy of scarcity that replaced nature's abundance when we abandoned our hunter-gatherer ways for a controlled-resource economy.

A life based on maintaining secrets creates the need for endless cover-ups. We end up distancing ourselves from our Truth and our Circle. The harm comes not from the secret itself, but from the act of keeping a secret.

When we are able to let go of our secrets, we can more fully embrace life and those around us. To receive a person's secret, we draw upon our Truthlistening ability to show acceptance, support, and non-judgmental empathy. This is easier said than done when the secret involves us, as with the case with Addie back in chapter 3. She confronted her fears of uncleanliness and disconnection by disclosing to her camp mates that she had a sexually transmitted disease. Her healing came not only from sharing her Truth, but also from having it received by open Hearts.

There is a saying: *to know you is to love you*. The inverse is also true: *to be known is to be loved*. When we live from the Heart, we have a desire to share the dark, hidden, and contrary aspects of ourselves with those closest to us. It is the manifestation of a Truthspeaker's innate yearning to have no secrets.

If we are serious about fostering no illusions and abandoning hurtful patterns of behavior, we have nothing to fear and everything to gain by shedding our secrets. As Truthspeakers, we can begin relationships by inviting our new partners to talk with our previous partners. No matter what our past relationships entailed or how they ended up, they clearly reflect who we are and what we carry.

This chapter concludes Part IV of our return to Truth. In the following chapters, we envision what life could be when we invite others to rediscover their Truths with us. Truthspeaking might begin as a personal journey, yet its power and beauty only starts to fully shine when it begins to ripple through our lives and relationships.

Chapter Nineteen Endnotes

1   A.E. Kelly et al., (2001). "What Is It About Revealing Secrets That Is Beneficial?" *Personality and Social Psychology Bulletin* 27 (2001): 651–65.

2   S. Kennedy, J.K. Kiecolt–Glaser, and R. Glaser, "Social Support, Stress, and the Immune System," in *Social Support: An Interactional View* (New York: Wiley, 1990), 253–66.

3   L.A. Lillard and C.W. Panis, "Marital Status and Mortality: The Role of Health," *Demography* 33, no. 3 (1996): 313-27.

4   Sissela Bok, *Secrets: On the Ethics of Concealment and Revelation* (New York: Pantheon Books, 1982), 25-6.

5   A.E. Kelly and K.J. McKillop, (1996). "Consequences of Revealing Personal Secrets," *Psychological Bulletin* 120 (1996): 450–65.

6   D.G. Larson and R.L. Chastain, "Self–Concealment: Conceptualization, Measurement, and Health Implications," *Journal of Social and Clinical Psychology* 9 (1990): 439–55.

7   J. Macdonald and I. Morely, "Shame and Non–Disclosure: A Study of the Emotional Isolation of People Referred for Psychotherapy," *British Journal of Medical Psychology* 74 (2001): 1–21.

8   Robert R. Rodriguez and Anita E. Kelly, "Health Effects of Disclosing Secrets to Imagined Accepting Versus Nonaccepting Confidants." *Journal of Social and Clinical Psychology* 25, no. 9 (2006): 1023-47.

9   Mary Kawena Pukui, *'Ōlelo No'eau, Hawaiian Proverbs and Poetical Sayings*, 120.

PART FIVE

CREATING A TRUTHSPEAKING CULTURE

Knowing our Truth is one thing. Living it is quite another. In this final section of the book, we learn how to practically apply what we have learned in our daily lives. Those who have stepped through this threshold before us give us guidance by sharing the questions that arose for them.

The book concludes by distilling Truthspeaking to its essence. As you now know, the Voice of Truth is spoken with few words and much Heart. For that reason, the last chapter reflects the spirit of Heart-clarity by being the shortest one in the book. It gives us just what we need to begin creating the culture that both encourages and emanates Truth.

CHAPTER TWENTY

LIVING THE CULTURE

As we approach the end of this book, we come to the next phase of the Truthspeaking journey—living our Truth. To make that transition easier, I would like to share the questions regarding it that I am most often asked. They will serve as both a review and a reminder.

"What is the easiest way to begin Truthspeaking?"

Another variation of the question is, "When is it best to Truthspeak?" The answer to both is, "when there is Truth to speak." The term *Truthspeaking* is comprised of two words: *speak truth*. I suggest that you simply start with that directive, then follow the steps:

1. Speak directly, succinctly, and in the moment.
2. Make sure that you are speaking *your* Truth.
3. Speak to the point, without overtones or disguising a message.
4. Remember that thinking out loud is not Truthspeaking.
5. Envision Truthspeaking as the way William Penn in 1683 described the speech of the Lenni Lenape (Delaware) Indians: "short, elegant, fervent."[1]

"What's at the heart of a successful relationship based on Truthspeaking?"

Let's begin with the following Zen story:

A Beggar sitting beside the road asked a passing Sage for alms.

"Are you extravagant?" asked the Sage.

"Yes," replied the Beggar.

"Do you like lounging around drinking coffee and smoking?"

"Yes," again stated the Beggar.

"What about going to the hot springs every day?"

"Oh, yes."

"Also having a good time drinking with your friends?"

"I do like all of those things."

With a frown the Sage handed him a large gold coin.

Next to him was another Beggar, who also asked for alms.

"Are you extravagant?" asked the Sage.

"No," stated the Beggar.

"Do you like loafing around smoking and drinking coffee?"

"No I don't."

"Maybe you go often to the hot springs?"

"No."

"But do you go drinking with your friends?"

"I do not. I only want to live simply and meditate."

The Sage smiled and gave him a small copper coin.

"Why only this," whined the Beggar, "for a frugal Seeker devoted to his practice, when you were so kind to that loafer?"

His needs," the Sage replied, "were greater than yours."[2]

The guideline upon which all others hinge is to honor each person's Truth. The first Beggar in the story is centered in his Heart-of-Hearts and speaks his Truth, while the second Beggar is centered in his mind and speaks his preferences and prejudices. The Sage demonstrates the Zen concept of *no mind*: showing no preference or prejudice, he respects each Beggar's Truth, even though it might not be his.

"Is Truthspeaking the means or the end?"

It must be remembered that Truthspeaking is only the process; it is not the Truth itself. Truthspeaking alone cannot bring us to self-knowing or make our relationships work. Truthspeaking takes our presence, our passion—and sometimes our frustration—to make it work. And most of all, it takes trust and acceptance in whatever our Heartvoice says.

Our first responsibility is to acknowledge and speak our Truths to ourselves. We are speaking our Truths and listening to Truth in every moment, with every breath and movement. Everything we do is either speaking or listening. It is like a stream that is ever-flowing, in both directions at once. Our only choice in the matter is whether or not to recognize the flow and consciously involve ourselves in it. When we say, "Enough Truthspeaking for now," we are actually saying, "I'm not used to being myself; I have to go back to my facade for a while."

Our second responsibility is to speak our Truth in the Now, and our third responsibility is to speak it to whomever else is involved in our Truth. That last responsibility is seldom as easy as the first two. The person involved may not be present, there may be communication issues, or we may fear the consequences.

"How do I determine who to share my Truth with and how much of it should I tell?"

1. **First remember what Truthspeaking is *not*.** Truthspeaking is built upon empathetic listening, brevity, and clarity. It does *not* mean speaking in stream-of-conscience mode, or verbalizing every thought and feeling as it occurs, to whomever crosses our path.

2. **Second, be intentional about choosing your audience.** If you are feeling resentful toward someone, take your Truth directly to *him*. Talking to anyone else is more likely gossip than Truthspeaking. Ultimately, though, Truth

is personal; so only you can determine the appropriate audience for your Truth.

3. **Third, communicate your Truth using language your audience understands.** When explaining family finances to a ten year-old, choose terms and concepts that she can grasp. Consider having a language, cultural, or generational 'translator' speak for you or help you chose the right words. The long-term solution to some dysfunctional communication patterns goes beyond the realm of this book and may require the help of a professional counselor or mediator.

4. **Lastly, don't imperil yourself**. If sharing your Truth subjects you or someone else to pain or injury that you deem unjust, or if you are being exploited or manipulated, you may choose not to speak your Truth. When I find myself in such a situation, I typically still feel the need to speak my Truth as soon as possible, so I find an appropriate person.

TRUTH OF RELATIONS CHART

To help determine how to gear your Truthspeaking to your audience, take a look at the accompanying chart. It depicts all of our human relationships, from the most intimate at the center to the most casual at the perimeter.

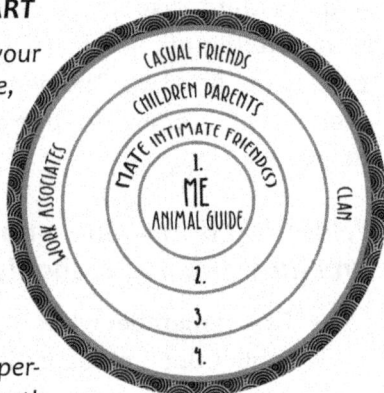

CASUAL FRIENDS
CHILDREN PARENTS
INTIMATE FRIENDS
MATE
1.
ME
ANIMAL GUIDE
WORK ASSOCIATES
CLAN
2.
3.
4.

To use the chart:

1. *Find the hoop number of the person who is involved in your Truth.*
2. *Speak your full Truth to that person, without reserve.*
3. *When you deem appropriate, you may speak the same Truth, without reserve, to anyone in a lesser-numbered hoop.*
4. *The higher numbered the hoop in which the person dwells, the less details of your Truth it may be appropriate or necessary for them to hear.*

To show how the Hoop of Relations works, let's say I am having a conflict with my brother. I would speak my Truth regarding that conflict clearly and completely with him, because he is directly involved. If my mate were my trusted confidant, I could also share my Truth completely with her, because she is in a smaller-numbered hoop. If anything, I might share only the basic facts of this Truth with my boss at work, and only if it was necessary and appropriate, because he is further out on the Hoop of Relations than where the Truth dwells.

"Is it ever okay to repeat my Truth?"

If someone challenges your Truth or tries to get you off topic, you might be able to help by repeating your Truth—but only the plain Truth and nothing but the Truth. However, you should only reprise it once, as anything further often feeds behaviors that keep the person from hearing.

"Can I Truthspeak with someone much older or younger than me?"

A former student told me the following story of what occurred when he was guiding a group of 16 on an outdoor adventure in the mountains of France: "During one discussion about Truthspeaking, a pilot told us that this way of communication is a vital part of their training. They have to express feelings, doubts, and opinions in the moment because both pilots are monitoring one another. It doesn't matter how much older and more experienced the other pilot is. If you are 21 and a rookie but still have a gut feeling something isn't going right—or the experienced pilot may not be doing something quite right—it needs to be talked about. He also told us that most accidents or problems while flying are caused by friction in communication between the crew."

Remember that Truthspeaking is one Heart connecting with another. While age may be a factor informing our conversation, it ought not hinder us from sharing Truth.

"How do I Truthspeak with large groups?"

The same way you would Truthspeak with an individual. The best presenters make each audience member feel as though he is being personally addressed. Yet speaking in front of large groups can be a depersonalizing experience for both the speaker and audience members. The solution for the speaker is to change perspective.

The most effective communication—that which closes the gap between Hearts—is one-on-one. Half of the equation is already there: you are one person. Your challenge is to transform your audience from a faceless crowd into the other person. If you can do your part, each audience member will do hers. After all, each of them came not to be part of an amorphous audience, but to connect with you. Two tricks can help here:

1. **Choose one person in the audience** who is resonating with you and address your talk to him.
2. **Start with a personal story** that establishes a Heart connection between you and your audience.

Once you have established that one-on-one relationship, you should find it much easier to speak your truth. Your natural tendency to feel naked and vulnerable in front of a large group will dissolve. You will be able to share your soul just as though you were sitting with someone in your living room, and each audience member will go home feeling as though she knows you.

"Do you have any advice for shy speakers?"

Shyness can have many causes, which could be intrinsic, adopted, or imposed. Whatever the case, if you are shy, you may find yourself often struggling to speak your Truth. And struggling is the antithesis of spontaneity, which is foundational to Truthspeaking.

If you are like most shy people, you perceive yourself as having a performance boundary that you need to struggle through, which makes you all the more self-conscious than you already are. Rather than dealing with the boundary, try this:

- Tell yourself that this is about you, not about how other people are going to react.

- Embrace the essence of what you want to say, without trying to formulate it perfectly by going over and over it.

- Assume that what you say is going to make sense. If someone does not understand, it is his responsibility to ask for clarification.

- Most importantly, just get it out.

"How do I stay motivated to speak my Truth?"

Truthspeaking is such a far-reaching topic, and so countercultural, that some people become overwhelmed by it. For others, the return to Truth precipitates intense healing journeys. Deep woundedness can surface, or hard struggles with entrenched behavioral patterns and reactive egos can ensue.

As is typical with ventures into the unknown, the first step takes the most courage and focus, then the trek gets progressively easier. Still, as you get better at Truthspeaking, you are bound to hit a wall now and then. When that occurs, be wary of the externalizing (blaming something outside of yourself) trap.

Truth is personal, so it is important to own what works *and* what does not work. The latter point may seem counterintuitive regarding motivation, but it is your so-called failures that point right where you need to go in order to improve your Truthspeaking skills. When something doesn't go right for me, the first thing I do is express my gratitude for the learning opportunity. To get back on track, I then recall my reasons for wanting to return to Truth.

Some of the reasons workshop participants have given for wanting to stay focused on Truthspeaking are to:

- Accept my Truth without being victimized by it.

- Allow others to have their own feelings.

- Read my feelings and emotions more clearly, so that I can share them.

- Learn how to avoid projecting my feelings onto others, to try to control or change them.

- Get over my fear of being spontaneous, and just let people know me as I am.

As you'll find, the journey back to Truth is a return to the soul of your being—to what you already know and who you already are. Yet even with that motivation, you can end up feeling overwhelmed. After all, you who have not been raised as a Truthspeaker are essentially restructuring the way you communicate.

Fortunately, you have another powerful reason—perhaps the most powerful—to go forward: the coming generations. If you can transform the legacy of Truth suppression that you have inherited, you will allow them to grow up as Truthspeakers. They will then have an excellent chance of being more empowered individuals, having stronger relationships, and being better Earth stewards than if they were relegated to the sad tradition you are abandoning.

The Chapter at a Glance

The key to beginning Truthspeaking is found in the term's root words, which form the directive: *speak Truth*. We begin by learning to speak directly, succinctly, and in the moment. We make sure that what we speak is our Truth, and we speak it both succinctly and directly, without manipulative overtones or a disguised message. We remember that the guideline upon which all others hinge is: honor each person's Truth, even when it appears to run contrary to our own.

Truthspeaking is only the process; it is not the Truth itself. Speaking our Truth alone cannot bring us to self-knowing or make our relationships work. It takes our presence, our passion—and sometimes our frustration. And most of all, it takes trust in whatever our Heartvoice speaks.

Our first responsibility is to acknowledge and speak our Truth to our self. We are speaking and listening to Truth in every moment, with every breath and movement. All that we do is either speaking or listening. It is like a stream that is ever-flowing, in both directions at once. Our only choice is whether or not to recognize the flow and consciously engage in it. When we say, "Enough Truthspeaking for now," we are actually saying, "I'm not used to being myself; I have to go back to my facade for a while."

Our second responsibility is to speak our Truth in the Now, and to whomever else is involved in that Truth. It's not always the easiest thing to do, as the person involved may not be present, there may be communication issues, or we may fear the consequences. Above all, it is important that we feel safe and share with the appropriate person.

Truthspeaking is about empathetic listening, brevity, and clarity. It is *not* about stream-of-conscience talking to anyone and everyone. We should be intentional about choosing the audience for our Truth, and communicate it in language they understand. At times, we may want to consider having a language, cultural, or generational "translator" speak for us. In some cases, it may be necessary to seek the help of a professional counselor or mediator.

If sharing your Truth subjects you or someone else to unjust pain or injury, or if you are being exploited or manipulated, you are justified in choosing not to speak your Truth in that moment. When we find ourselves in such a situation, the appropriate follow-up is typically to speak the Truth of the situation as soon as possible to an appropriate person.

For some of us, the return to Truth will foment intense healing journeys. Deep woundedness may reveal itself, or we may become aware of the fact that we have entrenched dysfunctional relational patterns or belligerent egos. As with most ventures into the unknown, the first step takes the most courage and focus, then it gets progressively easier. Still, we should expect to hit a wall now and then.

Truth is personal, so it is important to take responsibility for what works *and* what does not work. It is our so-called failures that point us precisely to where we need to go in order to improve our Truthspeaking skills.

Fortunately, we have a powerful—perhaps the most powerful—motivator: the coming generations. If they can grow up as Truthspeakers, they will have every opportunity to be empowered individuals with strong, healthy relationships and the ability to care kindly for our Earthen Home.

Chapter Twenty Endnotes

1   *William Penn's Own Account of the Lenni Lenape or Delaware Indians*, ed. Albert Cook Myers (New Jersey: Middle Atlantic Press, 1970), 43.

2   Idries Shah, *The Subtleties of the Inimitable Mulla Nasrudin* (London: The Octagon Press, 1983), 6-7.

THE CULTURE'S HEART

Early in this book, I shared these words from Chief Joseph: "It does not require many words to speak the truth." I'd now like to close the book by showing that neither does it require many words to speak *about* Truth. Upon completion of the Teaching Drum Outdoor School's Wilderness Guide Program, I asked my ten students to sum up what they learned about Truthspeaking from their intense experience of living together in an isolated wilderness camp for a full year. Here is the document they created:

How to Truthspeak

- Get in touch with your Truth.
- Express it clearly and concisely.
- Do it without delay.

How to Truthlisten

- Be open and accepting.
- Give acknowledgment.
- Give encouragement.

They not only expressed their deep understanding of Truthspeaking, but they presented this whole book in under thirty words. I realized right away that if we can take those few and precious words to Heart, it is all we need. For a constant reminder, I have them posted on my living room wall. If you would like to do the same, you'll find a copy-ready version on the next page, or you can upload it from the Snow Wolf Publishing webpage.

On the page after next is an even more concise version of the book. Over my front door is a small banner that says *Honor and Respect*. The expression comes from the Native Elders who have guided me in the ways of Truthspeaking since I was seven years of age. With the Elders drawing from countless generations of experience with Truthspeaking, I'm not surprised that they could encapsulate it even more succinctly than my students did. Along with the copy-ready version included here, you can find it on the Snow Wolf Publishing webpage.

With our time together coming to an end, I would like to make a special request. After you have reawakened to the Elder-wisdom found in this book, will you please pass it on to someone else who might gain from it? The Elders reminded me often enough that keeping *Honor and Respect* alive in my Heart is the only thing I need, so I feel comfortable recommending the same for you. After all, your Heartvoice comes not from this book, but rather from what you hold and cherish deep within.

The collective Heart-center for Native people is the Drum. The Ojibwe in my area call the Drum *Dewe'igan*,[1] which has *o-De*, their word for Heart,[2] at its root. When Drum speaks, the Native person hears the call to come together and hear her Voice of Truth. At the same time, the Drum brings the community's heartbeats into alignment with the heartbeat of the Earth Mother. My greatest hope is that when visiting these pages you have heard the voice of the Drum, and that it will continue to reverberate through you.

Chapter Twenty-One Endnotes

1 "dewe'igan," *The Ojibwe People's Dictionary*, last modified 2015, accessed 25 April 2019, https://ojibwe.lib.umn.edu/main-entry/dewe-igan-na.

2 "ode'," *The Ojibwe People's Dictionary*, last modified 2015, accessed 25 April 2019, https://ojibwe.lib.umn.edu/main-entry/ode-nid.

HOW TO TRUTHSPEAK

· Get in touch with your Truth ·

· Express it clearly and concisely ·

· Do it without delay ·

HOW TO TRUTHLISTEN

- • BE OPEN AND ACCEPTING •
- • GIVE ACKNOWLEDGMENT •
- • GIVE ENCOURAGEMENT •

HONOR AND RESPECT

THE WISDOM KEEPERS

I consider some books to be my Elders. Were it not for the diligence of a few dedicated People who asked the Old Ones to
leave their wisdom-tracks behind on paper, much of our Indigenous Ways would be lost to us.

Unfortunately, some of those dedicated People were self-
serving mercenaries and proselytizers attempting to lure the
Native to the plow and the pulpit. Still, what they preserved can
help us return to the healing ways of the Circle and the Truth of
the Now. My favorite Native-language dictionary was written by
a European cleric sent to capture the language and bring it back
home, so that it could be taught to aspiring missionaries. They
then came equipped with religious hymns and texts made all the
more alluring because they were translated into the indigenous
language.

That's history. We also have contemporary books that the
voices of the Old Ones echo through. I Honor the authors of
those books as well, and following are some that I recommend
for your further exploration of Truthspeaking and related topics:

Anger by Thich Nhat Hanh

Fear by Thich Nhat Hanh

The Evasion English Dictionary by Maggie Balistreri

*Gossip: Ten Pathways to Eliminate It from Your Life and Trans-
form Your Soul* by Laurie Palatnik with Bob Berg

The Healing Power of Humor by Allen Klein

How to get from where you are to where you want to be by
Cheri Huber

The Power of Now by Eckhart Tolle

A New Earth by Eckhart Tolle

Radical Honesty: How to Transform your Life by Telling the Truth by Brad Blanton

Nonviolent Communication: A Language of Life by Marshall Rosenberg

Start where You Are by Pema Chodron

Don't Bite the Hook: Finding Freedom from Anger, Resentment and Other Destructive Emotions by Pema Chodron

Working with Anger by Thubten Chodron

Original Instructions: Indigenous Teachings for a Sustainable Future edited by Melissa K. Nelson

The Original Instructions: Reflections of an Elder on the Teachings of the Elders, Adapting Ancient Wisdom to the Twenty-First Century by Manitonquat

Journey to the Ancestral Self by Tamarack Song. Note in particular the *Belief and Debwewin* and *'Chi Debwewin* sections in the *Spiritual Attunement* chapter

Whispers of the Ancients: Native Tales for Teaching and Healing in Our Time, by Tamarack Song

Song of Trusting the Heart: A Classic Zen Poem for Daily Meditation by Tamarack Song

Zen Rising: 366 Sage Stories to Enkindle Your Days by Tamarack Song

GLOSSARY

Balance: The state of personal centeredness that results from following inner guidance and living in harmony with life.

(Out of) Balance: The state of internal and environmental disharmony caused by an ego-based existence.

Circle Consciousness: Heart-generated thinking and feeling that takes into account the Hoop of Relations. Allows transcendence of the Ego, to accommodate the needs of others along with personal needs.

Circle Way: The manner in which all things are related to, and affect, each other.

Circumstances: The neutral background information upon which a Truthspeaking interchange is based. Typically necessitates the redefinition of facts as observations.

Civilized: The lifestyle, and its People, that result from living out of balance with the Hoop of Relations. Characterized by isolation from Nature, environmental degradation, regimentation, hierarchical structures, materialism, and loss of individuality.

Consensus: The collective Truth resulting from an integrative process where everyone's voice is heard, honored, and incorporated.

Contrary Thought: The result of the ego's voice, which often seems to run in opposition to the Heartvoice. Not related to the deliberate confoundings of a traditional-culture contrarian, heyoka, court jester, or satirist.

Core Emotions: They are *fear* and *longing*, and they lie at the root of emotional expression. When they go unexpressed, they can manifest as **Reactive Feelings**.

Elder An aged community or clan member who is typically highly regarded as a bearer of inter-generational clan knowledge, a keeper of traditions, and a source of guidance based on wisdom drawn from life experience and ancestral memories.

Empathy The recognition of another's feelings and the Truth behind them. Goes beyond sympathy and compassion, which have us vicariously experiencing another's feelings without the related Truth. Empathy is what transforms active listening into Truthlistening.

Fearspeaking Expressing for manipulative or self protective purposes. Based on half-truths, along with words and gestures that are devoid of genuine respect, though they may mimic it.

Green Season The warm portion of a snowcountry Native's two-season year.

Heart-of-Hearts A person's center of Balance and source of Personal Truth. The seat of Wisdom and guide for actions that are in attunement with the Hoop of Relations.

Heartvoice The expression of the Heart-of-Hearts, which is spoken and heard by the entire physical-mental-emotional being.

Heart-to-Heart listening/speaking (a.k.a. *intuitive listening/ speaking, Naturespeak*) The First Language—the mother tongue of all life and the foundation of intra and inter-species communication.

Hoop of Relations (a.k.a. *Web of Life, Hoop of Life, Life-Circle,* and other variations) The community of Plant, Animal, Mineral and Sky beings who live together in Balance.

Intuitive mind (a.k.a. *limbic system, mid-brain, mammalian brain, the subconscious*) The seat of long-term memory, emotions, sensory processing, and deep guidance.

Native Someone who lives a subsistence or hunter-gatherer lifestyle. Also the lifestyle itself.

Personal Frontier The realm of possibility that exists when one embraces fear as his guide, then steps beyond convention and familiarity..

Personal Truth An expression of the Heart-of Hearts, which stands above reproach because it is valid for the individual—and only the individual—who speaks it.

Rational mind (a.k.a. *neocortex, new brain , primate brain*) The seat of deliberate and analytical thought.

Reactive Feelings The result of **Core Emotions** going unexpressed. Include anger, jealousy, guilt, resentment, frustration, and despair.

Respectful Speaking Communication that is free of guilt, expectation, or judgment. An effective way to defuse and transform disrespect.

Shadowing A silent speech and movement-mimicking exercise, used for sensitizing and developing listening skills.

Talking Circle A group dialogue where each individual has the opportunity to speak on a given subject and has the undivided attention of the group. The general intention is to transcend pure self-interest and speak from the perspective of **Circle Consciousness.**

Truthlistening (a.k.a. *empathetic listening, intuitive listening*) Holding calm, receptive, nonjudgmental space for a speaker, to encourage and support the expression of her Truth.

Truthspeaking Concise, straight-from-the-heart expression of personal reality. Engenders trust and strengthens relationship.

Voice of the Ancestors (a.k.a. *Ancestral Memories*) Guidance from our forebears, which we have accrued along our evolutionary path. May be genetically imprinted. Accessed through dreams, intuition, and ritual experiences. Often appears in the guises of metaphor and story.

White Season The cold, snowy portion of a of a snowcountry Native's two-season year.

Ojibwe Terms

Bizindan Ostensibly means *listen,* yet in a deeper sense it means **Truth**, for when one listens with his Heart, he hears the Truth in all things.

Debwewin Means *Truth,* and at the same time it means *listen,* for there is no Truth without listening.

Giizis Miikana The Sun Trail, which is the sacred path of the Sun, the Moon, the yearly seasons, and the seasons of our lives. When one listens to her **Heartvoice,** she hears an echo of the Giizis Miikana,

Ode Heart. Can refer to either the organ or the **Heart-of-Hearts.**

Odena Village; or literally, *place of many hearts.* Recognizes the Heart as a person's and a community's center.

To learn more about Tamarack Song's work, please visit these sites:

www.healingnaturecenter.org

Where Towering Pine and Whispering Breeze
Revitalize body, mind, and spirit
Release pain, stress, and sorrow
Renew relationship with all of life

www.teachingdrum.org

Where Wilderness is the classroom,
Ancient Voices are the teachers,
knowing self and Balance is the quest

www.snowwolfpublishing.org

Our mission is to publish relevant, well-crafted books
that help nurture and heal the connection
between humans and the natural world
and to be a guide for future generations

ABOUT THE AUTHOR

When Tamarack was a child, he got to regularly practice Truthspeaking with the wild animals in the extensive woods and wetlands that comprised his backyard. As a young man, he lived for several years with a pack of Wolves. After that, he learned the human nuances of Truthspeaking from Menominee, Ojibwe, Blackfoot, Hopi, Iroquois, Australian Aboriginal, and Maygar Elders. They taught him much of the terminology and phrasing found in this book. He augmented this organic tutelage with his lifelong academic study of nature, language, anthropology, and indigenous cultures.